DARTMOOR
wildern

...Dartmoor ...ce the 1960s when he fell in love with its grandeur and beauty as a schoolboy.

Since that time he served for over 30 years as a police officer, mainly in the West Devon and Dartmoor area. During that time, almost 20 years was spent in the Dartmoor Rescue Group, for which he was awarded an MBE in 1997. He has since retired and is now a Dartmoor National Park Guide, sharing his enthusiasm and love for the moors with visitors and locals alike.

He has written numerous books about Dartmoor, its infamous prison, industrial archaeology and he regularly contributes to local Dartmoor based magazines and publications.

Simon has appeared on television and radio and is now much in demand throughout the West Country as a guest speaker for community organisations. He lives on the edge of Dartmoor in Tavistock with his family, and spends his free time as a guide on Lundy Island as well as climbing in the Lake District, the Alps and the Himalayas.

These guided walks are taken from a series written for the Dartmoor News over several years, apart from the last walk involving the East to West two-day walk.

Positive feedback received from those articles led to this small volume, of some of the most enjoyed perambulations, being made available under one cover.

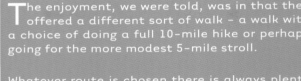

The enjoyment, we were told, was in that they offered a different sort of walk – a walk with a choice of doing a full 10-mile hike or perhaps going for the more modest 5-mile stroll.

Whatever route is chosen there is always plenty to see on the journey. This book is intended as a guide in the true sense, to be taken with you and used out 'in the field' so to speak, to use in order to guide you across some of the most beautiful ground that Dartmoor has to offer.

As with all guides there is no substitute for the ability to use a map and compass.

It is highly recommended that such skills are possessed before venturing out into the heart of the moors where the weather can change quickly and the walker can find himself lost in no time at all.

DARTMOOR
wilderness walks

Much of northern Dartmoor lies well within the Military Ranges. The information concerning checking firing times must be followed to avoid venturing onto the ranges during live firing days. Do not touch any suspicious metal objects while walking within the range areas.

Military firing times information can be found at: www.dartmoor-ranges.co.uk or by phone on: 0800 458 4868. Firing times are also broadcast frequently on BBC Radio Devon.

Every effort has been made to check access availability, but conditions can change with little notice after publication. We would welcome being updated on any changes affecting the chosen routes or in respect to any inaccuracies that might have managed to sneak their way into the text unnoticed.

There are greater, larger and more concise guides available but it is hoped that this modest effort will simply cater for those walkers who have asked for the popular series to be consolidated into a small volume.

The publishers hope that as much pleasure is derived from this guide as it was when the routes were walked and written-up in the planning stage.

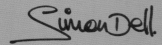

DARTMOOR wilderness walks...

index

DARTMOOR
wilderness walk 01

The Plym Valley and Drizzlecombe

Length: Choice of a 5-mile walk or a 10-mile walk
Start: The small parking area at the end of the 'no-through' lane leading from Sheepstor Village
Grid ref: SX578 678
Difficulty: Moderate for the 5-mile route and arduous for the 10-mile option due to long grass

Either a 10-mile or 5-mile walk. The 5-mile route is easy to follow with various features but the 10-mile walk has a section across open moorland so the ability to use a map and compass would be essential, especially in poor visibility. This walk starts at the small parking area at grid reference SX578 678 at the end of the 'no-through' lane leading from Sheepstor Village.

From the parking area, walk towards Gutter Tor until you reach **Edward's Path** - a rough track with Gutter Tor on your right side. There are views ahead of you to Hen Tor, which takes the form of a sharp prominent triangular peak on the south side of the River Plym.

1. Gutter Tor Car park: SX578 67
2. Dits. Warren House: SX583 662
3. Plym Ford: SX610 684
4. Broad Rock: SX618 671
5. Duck's Pool: SX625 679
6. Eylesbarrow: SX599 686

As you walk on the track there is plenty of evidence below you on the left of the work of the tinners, with their streaming works, with parallel mounds of spoil from their quest for tin in the valley. The whole of this area was also used for the breeding of rabbits, hence the name given to the area of **Ditsworthy Warren.** [SX583 662].

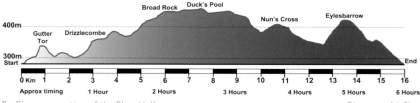

Profile cross section of the Plym Walk.

Distance: 16.2km
Total ascent and descent: 389m

The Plym Valley and Drizzlecombe

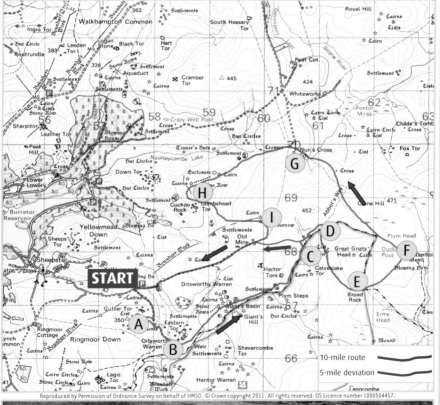

Reproduced by Permission of Ordnance Survey on behalf of HMSO. © Crown copyright 2011. All rights reserved. OS Licence number 1000504457.

10-mile route
5-mile deviation

START

2

Ditsworthy Warren House

To try to keep down the vermin (mainly stoats etc) the warreners built traps of granite and wood, the ruined remains of which are still to be seen around the valley on your left. We are heading along the track to see one of these traps, which is situated on the slopes of Gutter Tor (A). [SX577 688]

Ahead you might, if the weather is clear, have a good view of the ridge in the distance of **Trowlsworthy** slightly over to the right – the site of another Warren. **Hen Tor**, also a Warren, and **Langcombe Head** and **Shavercombe** are also on the south side of the River Plym.

Just as the path goes around a sharp left hand bend into the gully, turn right and go uphill, back towards the summit of Gutter Tor on a gentle grassy slope leading to the top of the tor. As you go up the path between the bracken, you will see that your route enters an area of boulders and you come across a wall ruin, which crosses the pathway. Look to your left beside the path and you will see a large boulder put up onto its side to form a funnelling wall which leads into the vermin trap about 8 paces from the path. [SX579 666] The trap is capped with a granite slab and is only a few feet from the track path. A small diversion here, to the north, takes you to a recently discovered stone which is believed to be the remains of a carved stone cross lying on its side about a hundred meters away.

Now return back down to **Edwards Path,** and to the bend, as the track goes down into the tinners' gully in the direction of **Ditsworthy Warren House.** [SX583 662]. The track leads you through what would have been a gate and into the enclosure of Ditsworthy Warren (B). [SX583 662]

Vermin Trap on Gutter Tor

Ahead and to your left you will see the old warren house start to appear. Through the fields left and right you will see the mounds of the man-made rabbit warrens, which housed the rabbits, known as burries or pillow mounds locally. The track leads you to the house, now a training centre bunkhouse for expeditions. As you approach the house, pass it on your right and continue to the rear where you will see several dog kennels built into the field walls. Looking south across the River Plym the views of the **Hen Tor Warren** are particularly fine, with evidence of large pillow mounds of the warreners in the area, along with field boundaries.

Follow along the track with the Plym Valley Way over to your right until you reach the significant **Drizzlecombe Stone Rows** C [SX591 669] one of the largest standing stones on Dartmoor, that marks the end of one of the rows.

Ditsworthy kennel

Once you have explored the stone row, take a look at the nearby **cairn** then walk downhill towards the River Plym. We are now going to turn to walk up the Plym valley where you will see what affect the tinners had in this area. Ahead of you and to the south of the river there are some large settlement circles. You will find a reasonable path beside the river and also a few yards from it. Ahead and up the valley you will see **Lower Hartor Tors.**

The valley becomes boggy in a number of places so keep to the left and go around the wet areas using the high ground. **Evil Combe** [SX605 677] is particularly wet and worth avoiding. Continue up the Plym until you reach another smaller combe on your left. Turn left into the small valley and head for some old ruins, which are situated on a track at the head of the combe D.
This is where the 5-mile walkers turn left and westwards along the clearly defined path on their return journey back to the cars, via the Eylesbarrow mine ruins. The track is well defined all the way to Eylesbarrow where it joins the main track from Sheepstor to Princetown, and where the 10-mile route rejoins it.

Broad Rock

The 10-mile route walkers, however, turn right and eastwards along the well defined track to Plym Ford [SX610 684] where we cross the river Plym, now a much smaller stream, and follow the less discernable route of the Abbot's Way. Depending on the season, the path is reasonably well worn, but it would be wise to take a compass bearing for **Broad Rock** at **SX618673**, which is our next destination (E). The rock itself is becoming quite worn and careless walkers are eroding the inscription. There are a number of large rocks on this flat hilltop location, but the Broad Rock is the slightly larger oval one about knee high. There are fine views, if the weather is favourable, down the River Erme into Erme Pits as well as towards the distinctive pyramid-shaped spoil heap at the head of the Red Lake tramway to the southeast.

The next section of the route is best done on a compass bearing, for even in good weather **Duck's Pool,** our next destination, is in a hollow in a featureless landscape. As you approach, a narrow well-worn footpath takes you through some large rocks to the **letter box at William Crossing's memorial,** located under a large boulder about 5 feet high on the southern edge of the depression. (F)

After recording your presence in the visitors' book and enjoying the possibility of a break here, you now face a walk north westwards through the bottom of the boggy area of the pool. It is well worth a diversion by sticking with the well-worn path around the west side of the depression until you reach the other side. A brief check using a back bearing to Crossing's memorial will ensure you are on course for **Nun's Cross Farm,** [SX606 698] about 3 kilometres to our northwest.

Your route will take you across the top of **Plym Head** and the side of **Crane Hill** towards the **North Hessary radio mast,** seen way in the distance if the weather is clear. On the way keep an eye out for a **4-foot high pyramid rock with a tiny bronze cross** on the top.

This is **Northmore's Cross** and one of the smallest on Dartmoor. Nun's Cross Farm itself is now used as a bunkhouse for adventure training and walkers. While you are at the building put your back to the door and look back at the route you have just walked.

Duck's Pool

Look slightly to the right at the boundary wall of the farm enclosure and you might see a rather curious and carved stone in the wall, the purpose of which nobody is quite sure! You will have crossed the **Devonport Leat** not far from where it goes underground into the hillside to your left. We will rejoin the Leat on the other side of the hill once we have been to the farm G .

Once you have been to the farm and the ruins of the original farm by the trees it is worth a small diversion to visit **Nun's Cross,** *(or properly known as Siward's Cross)* [SX604 699] situated on the boundary of the farm's fields to the northwest.

The cross is over 6 feet high and located on a well-defined track from Princetown up to **Eylesbarrow Mines** [SX598 682]. **If you feel you would like to cut your walk slightly shorter** you may, if you wish, use this track to make your way up to Eylesbarrow which will save you about an hour in time.

For those sticking to the route from the cross, head westwards and through some

The illusive small Bronze Cross on Hand Hill

mining gullies to the point where the Devonport Leat comes flowing out of the tunnel in the hillside below you. Stick to the south of the Leat and head in a westerly direction over the hillside towards **Down Tor,** 2 kilometres ahead of you. We are going to visit the stone row, which leads up the slope towards the direction of the tor. This is one of the better examples of stone rows on the moors H . [SX587 692]

Drizzlecombe Stone Row

Once visited, leave the stone row and turn southeast towards Eylesbarrow Mine ruins on the hilltop ahead of you.

You will be dropping down into a small valley with **Combeshead Tor** to your right, on the other side of the enclosure wall. The valley can be a bit boggy but if you stick to the wall it will lead you to a reasonable crossing place.

Once over the stream head up to **Eylesbarrow Mine** (**I**), slightly to the right of the top of the hill. As you get nearer there are two old granite gateposts to help you to locate the mine ruins. It is worth spending a little while here looking around, but beware of some of the deeper holes and recently collapsed, but fenced, shafts.

This is where the 5-mile route joins the walk again. The route follows the main track southwest back to where you left your car some hours ago.

Open shaft at Eylesbarrow

The Devonport Leat

Shipley Bridge

Length: Choice of a 5-mile walk or a 10-mile walk
Start: Car park at Shipley Bridge
Grid ref: SX681 629
Difficulty: Moderate for both 5 and 10-mile routes. Open moorland with some tracks, some river crossings but no stiles

Follow the Zeal Tor Tramway up to the Balla Brook then into the Middle Brook valley to Uncle Ab's House. Onto Petre's Cross then Red Lake, Huntingdon and return via the Avon Dam and Rider's Rings.

Park at **Shipley Bridge car park,** 3 miles north of South Brent in front of the remains of the **19th century Industrial Works,** where naphtha was distilled from the moorland peat. The site was later used as a clay settling plant. Use the footpath leading past the public conveniences until you reach the road that leads to the **Avon Dam** following the **Avon River.**

1. Shipley Bridge:
2. Red lake:
3. Snowdon:
4. Huntingdon Cross:
5. Rider's Rings:
6. Black Tor:

Grid
SX681 62
SX646 670
SX668 684
SX665 664
SX678 643
SX681 636

Follow this road for a short distance and you come across the **Hunter's Stone** on your left. The stone itself was moved to this location many years ago and is carved with the names of the masters of the local hunt. Continue along the road uphill and around the left bend towards the **Avon Dam Water Treatment Works plant** A . On a nice day there are fine views behind you towards Shipley Tor and to your left you have the ruins of the settling pits from the days of the China Clay extraction in the area.

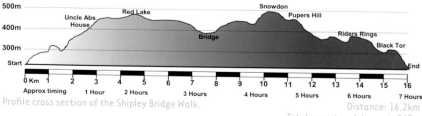

Profile cross section of the Shipley Bridge Walk.
Distance: 16.2km
Total ascent and descent: 562m

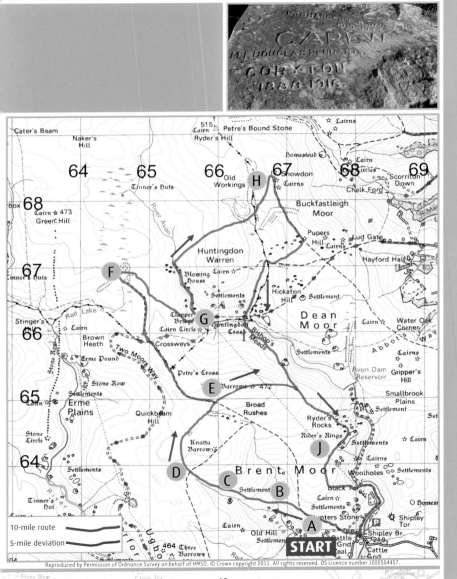

CAPEW
M.T. DOUGLAS PENNANT
CORYTON
1888-1916

Cater's Beam

Naker's Hill

515
Cairn
Ryder's Hill

Petre's Bound Stone

Cairns

64   65   66   Old Workings   67   Snowdon   68   Cairns   69
Circles
Scorriton
Down

box 68   Cairn ★ 473   Green Hill   Chalk Ford
Tinner's Huts   Buckfastleigh Moor

River Avon   Pupers Hill   Lud Gate   Cairns   Hayford Hall

67   Huntingdon Warren

Tinner's Huts   F   Blowing House   Cairn   Hickaton Hill   Settlement   Dean Moor   Water Oak Corner

Stinger's   Red Lake   Clapper Bridge   G   Huntingdon   Abbot's Way   Cairns
66   Cairn   Cairn Circle   Cross   Bishop's   Cairn
Brown Heath   Crossways   Meads   Settlements

Stone Row   Erme Pound   Two Moors Way   Petre's Cross   Avon Dam Reservoir   Gripper's Hill

65   Settlements   E   Barrows ★ 472   Smallbrook Plains
Erme Plains   Broad Rushes   Ryder's Rocks   Settlement

Stone Circle   Quickbeam Hill   Ryder's Rings   J   Cairn

64   Settlements   Knatta Barrow   Cairns   Woolholes   Settlements

D   Brent Moor   C   Settlement   B   Black Tor   Settlements

Tinner's Hut   A   Hunters Stone   Cairn   Shipley Tor   Homest

Cairn   Settlement   START   Shipley Br.

10-mile route
5-mile deviation

464   Old Hill   Settlement   Cattle Grid   Cattle Grid
Three Barrows   Crow Tor   Higher White Tor

10

Upon reaching the cattle grid leading into the Water Treatment Works do not enter the site but follow the right hand wall. On your right in the gorse bushes you will see the

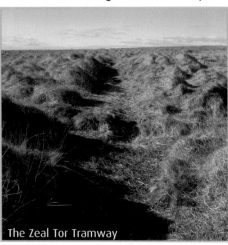

The Zeal Tor Tramway

track of an old tramway that takes you up on the westerly side of **Brent Moor** towards **Red Lake.** This is the ruin of the **Zeal Tor Tramway,** built in 1847 to take peat from Redlake down to Shipley Bridge. This venture failed after a short while, but in 1877 the naphtha buildings at Shipley were reused for processing china clay from Bala Brook head, a venture which also failed.

Continue to follow the wall until it goes around a sharp turn to the left downhill into the valley of the Balla Brook heading towards **Red Brook foot** **B** where the tree lined Red Brook comes down on the opposite hillside and joins the Bala Brook. Way in the distance to your west we can see **Wakka Tor** and **Ugborough Beacon.**

There are a variety of paths, which will assist you in crossing the slope. Ahead on a fine day you can see up the valley of the **Middle Brook** as it flows down into the Bala Brook and way into the distance. On a clear day you might be able to see the ruins of mine workings that you will be visiting shortly.

Looking into the valley of the Bala Brook there is a fine Bronze Age enclosure [SX672 630] down on your left, which has a fence around it. Instead of going right down to the river, turn to the right and follow the river upstream until the Middle Brook joins the Bala Brook from the other side of the valley.

Your path now crosses the Bala Brook and follows up the right bank of the Middle Brook. There is a good crossing point at the junction under some trees. Continue up the Middle Brook to the ruins of some old tin workings [SX662 635] - this is known as **Middle Brook Old Wheelhouse** **C** and provided power to a nearby mine. The views to the south from this location are magnificent and reach to the sea off South Devon.

Your journey continues up the Middle Brook through tinners' spoil heaps and turns to the right into the gully that leads up to the ruins of **Uncle Ab's House [SX656639]** Ⓓ.

Not much of it left now but it was far less ruinous in 1954 when the door lintel was still standing and there was a stone nearby with the inscription - CB 1809, suggesting perhaps that Uncle Ab's house was built in 1809 - years before the Zeal Tor tramway. It used to stable horses for the Zeal Tor tramway that took peat from Redlake down to Shipley Bridge, but it was originally used to stable packhorses for the peat workings nearby and there are the remains of a paddock in front of the house.

After Uncle Ab's house continue up through the valley passing spoil heaps and follow a distinct path uphill in the direction of the large pond at the top of the hill, only ten minutes from Uncle Abs House. From here we have a view up the Erme Valley towards Broad Rock, which we visited on our previous excursion. **It is here that the five and ten mile paths separate** with the five-mile route heading off to Eastern Whitabarrow [SX665 652] in the distance. The ten-mile route will eventually re-join the route near that location. The best route to take is to follow down to the dam at **Petre's Pits** where the wet area of the settling pits can be crossed using the path over the dam [SX658 648]. This is the deepened head of the Bala Brook and it is all that is left of three failed ventures

Uncle Ab's House

to extract poor quality china clay. The clay ran down in suspension along a series of pipes that took it to Shipley Bridge. Those on the five-mile route can now strike across the open moor, on a compass bearing in poor visibility, for the distinctive **Eastern White Barrow.**

The ten-mile route carries on north eastwards until you reach the route of the Zeal Tor Tramway coming up from the right and crossing your path. Turn left and head northwards along the tramway up to the damaged Bronze Age Cairn of the Western White Barrow and Petre's Cross [SX653 655]. Turf cutters from nearby Red Lake built themselves a shelter in the barrow and in so doing damaged the cairn. They knocked the arms off the old Petre's Cross and used it as a chimney breast. The views from here are superb on a good day - Plymouth, Salcombe, Torbay and much of Bodmin moor can be seen.

Looking to the north you will see the lonely pyramid of the Red Lake spoil tip at [SX646 670] **F** which is your next destination, reached by following the tramway then the old railway track.

Petre's Cross and cairn

Red Lake, with its distinctive landmark, lies in the heart of the Southern Moor and is the overgrown spoil tip of the China Clay works that started working in 1910 but had failed by 1933. The clay was water-blasted out from a deep pit and the slurry went to nearby settling beds at Greenhill. After a few days of settling, the sluices were opened and the clay in suspension flowed down pipes some 7 miles to the clay processing works near Ivybridge. The unwanted sand and gravel was loaded into trucks at Red Lake, which were then tipped onto the waste tip that we see today.

The railway, which ran alongside the clay pipes that led down to Ivybridge, was only used for moving people and basic materials and is known as the **Puffing Billy track.** It was 3ft gauge and small steam engines pulled passenger carriages. There are 3 deep pools, ruined buildings as well as the tip and is surrounded by mires and fen but is an interesting place to see.

Your route now takes you eastwards towards the Huntingdon Warren area. The rocks of Broad Falls [SX653 670] is not the easiest of places to cross the River Avon so it might be a good idea to divert slightly to negotiate the river at the clapper bridge [SX657 662] **G** . Once over the bridge a short walk upstream will lead you past a nice example of a ruined vermin trap by a tree, with its distinctive funnelling walls.

Clapper Bridge

Once at the ruined blowing house near Broad Falls [SX654 669] your course takes you northeast to the summit of Snowdon **H** [SX668 684], passing the distinctive 'T' Girt on your left.

From Snowdon a short walk brings you to **Pupers Hill [SX673 674]** then the ford [SX667 671] on the track leading to the ruined **Huntingdon Warren Farm,** which burnt down in 1956 and was only reached by a difficult track from Lud Gate. This farm started off being the focal point of an extensive rabbit warren business in the 19th century.

Your path now takes you downstream on the left bank to Keble Martin's chapel [SX666 666]. This was built in the early 20th century by a group of young men led by Keble Martin the famous botanist and sometime vicar of Dartington. The whitish granite pillar has a cross inscribed on it and just to the left of it is a step with the **Christian symbol PX** carved on it.

A short distance further is the ruined remains of an old tin ore-stamping floor of the Huntingdon Mine [SX665 664] where there is a derelict water wheel pit - part of the old tin mine of Devon Wheal Vor that closed down in 1815, but reopened for a short while in 1866 as the Huntingdon Mine. **Continue your way downhill to a modern-day Dartmoor curiosity:** the recently built, and useless, wall next to Huntingdon Cross **I** at [SX664 662], an essential part of an E.U. grant in this age of political correctness. What the 'old men' of the moors would have made of this beggars belief.

Your route crosses the ford on the Avon nearby and takes you south east across the hillside as you rise up walking parallel with the River until you see **Avon Dam** come into sight and over to your right you see **Eastern White Barrow** [SX665 652], a Bronze

Age cairn. It is a commanding structure - a streamlined heap of granite with a circular tower of stones. It looks rather like an early submarine, but is a burial structure. Continue around the hillside on one of the many pathways to the dwellings at **Ryder's Rings J** [SX678 643]. This is an extensive Bronze Age settlement with over 30 huts within a double pound ring as well as a great variety of animal enclosures of various sizes.

Keble Martin's Chapel

Across the hill you will see Black Tor [SX681 636] which signals the route back to Shipley Bridge. Continue to Black Tor which has some lovely rock features as well as pennyworts growing amongst its pitted walls.

At the tor look towards **Shipley Tor** across the valley with the distinctive wall leading to it, ahead of you will be seen a wall of an enclosure with rhododendrons growing, as well as a large dead tree. Head towards this wall and dead tree and follow it to the left. This will bring you down to the road which leads from Shipley Bridge up to the Avon Dam.

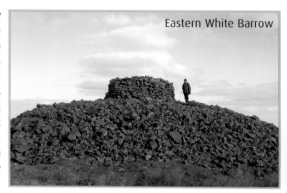

Eastern White Barrow

Once you have clambered down to the road, turn right and follow it back to the car park passing the ruins of Brent Moor House on your right and the Hunter's Stone, thence back to the **car part at the start of the walk.**

Black Tor

Hunter's Stone

Belstone to Hangingstone Hill

Length: Choice of a 5-mile walk or a 10-mile walk
Start: Belstone Village Car Park
Grid ref: SX621 938
Difficulty: Easy to moderate due to using so many tracks and paths for both routes. The 10-mile route can be boggy near Hangingstone.

Blue route: 10-mile route; into the valley of the River Taw follow the river upstream to Hangingstone Hill and return along the Oke Tor to Belstone Tor ridge.
Red route: 5-mile deviation; turn off early and going straight to Oke Tor, return the same way over Belstone Tor. This type of deviation can be done at numerous points along the walk to suit whichever length of walk you desire.

Some lanes, tracks and gates, as well as open moorland to cross. In poor visibility, especially on the Hangingstone Hill section of this walk, a map and compass are essential. There are also a number of streams to cross, not all have bridges.

1. Belstone Car park: SX621 93(
2. Knack Mine: SX614 884
3. Hangingstone Hill: SX619 861
4. Ted Hughes' memorial: SX609 865
5. Oke Tor: SX612 900
6. Belstone Tor: SX614 920

It is important to note that this walk enters the Okehampton Military Firing Range - it is essential to check the firing times and not to undertake this walk when live firing is taking place on the Okehampton Firing Range.

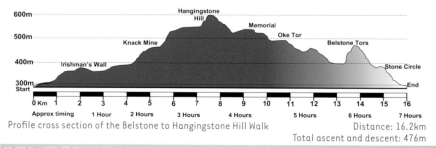

Profile cross section of the Belstone to Hangingstone Hill Walk

Distance: 16.2km
Total ascent and descent: 476m

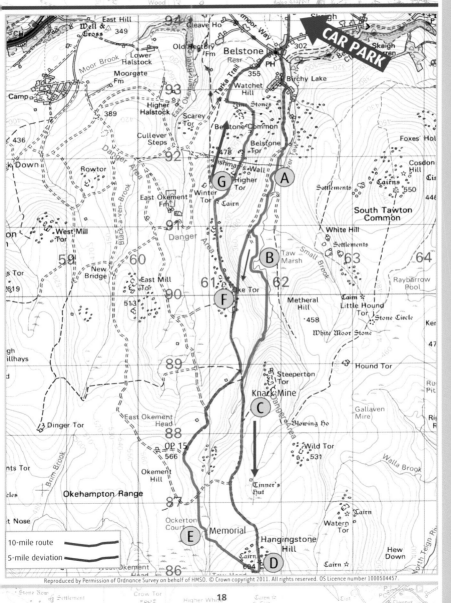

Belstone to Hangingstone Hill

CAR PARK

10-mile route

5-mile deviation

18

Park at the large village car park opposite the Belstone Village Hall [SX621 938]. From here, follow the road into the village, passing the old village stocks on your left. These are much restored, but remain as a sign of the discomforts endured by petty offenders up until the mid 19th Century. The road also passes a memorial standing stone where you fork left as you head out towards the valley of the River Taw and **Belstone Cleave** and the side of **Cosdon Beacon** on your left.

Belstone Stocks

The lane leads you past some cottages, passing by derelict tractors and agricultural machinery and eventually to the gate in the trees, which takes you out onto the open moors. This is the rough lane which allows vehicle access to the water works deep in the **Taw Valley** a few miles ahead. Follow this track, even though it might be uncomfortable in places, for if you take the worn paths on the left they all lead back to the main track.

Irishman's Wall

This track takes you into the large valley of the upper Taw River, passing the impressive **Irishman's Wall** (A) [SX618 918] coming down from the hillside on your right. An Irishman wishing to enclose that part of the moors reputedly built the wall in the early 19th Century. After allowing much of the work to be completed local moormen besieged the site and destroyed much of the wall causing the construction plans to be abandoned.

Ahead of you are views towards Steeperton Tor [SX618 887], looking like a pyramid with a narrow valley either side of it and even further in the distance to the right of Steeperton are glimpses of **Hangingstone Hill** [SX619 861] - much higher than the hills and tors around it.

To your left and across the River Taw rise other hills in this great amphitheatre, the side of **Cosdon Beacon** to your east, but whose summit is still illusive, further to its south lie the slopes of **Metheral Hill** to the left of Steeperton with **White Hill** and the slopes of **Little Hound Tor** a little further in the distance.

A little way after Irishman's Wall you will see a junction on your left which leads down to the River Taw and a large ford for military and farm vehicles, but continue on your path towards Steeperton Tor, walking parallel to the river. Ahead of you and to your right on the top of the ridge-line you will see **Oke Tor** [SX612 900].

Oke Tor

If you intend to do the 5-mile route you now need to start thinking about making your way up to this tor. Don't leave your ascent too late because the hill gets steeper the longer you leave it. You can easily pick out some fairly useful footpath tracks going up the hillside diagonally towards Oke Tor.

The main route will re-join you at Oke Tor after going on to, and back from, Hangingstone Hill. For those going on further up the valley path your route will depend upon how wet the ground is. If it is fairly dry then continue along the track until it peters out into a number of narrow footpaths which all lead into Steeperton Gorge [SX618 897] beside the river to the right of Steeperton Tor. If, however, the ground is wet then I would suggest going way over to the right and hug the lower slopes of the hillside to get to the gorge because the ground ahead of you can become quite boggy. *During the spring season there is a lovely show of the various bog-loving plants in the area, including the Sundews, Asphodels, Bog Cottons and Orchids.*

Whichever route you have chosen you will see about you the various odd looking constructions of the North Devon Water Board, as was built in the 1950s. These are the sink bore holes [SX606 916] taking water from the marshes to your left $\textcircled{B}$ to supply water to the Belstone Water Treatment Works and onwards to North Devon and Crediton.

The route now enters the narrow Steeperton Gorge, at the entrance of which is a pretty ford by some gateposts where herons are often to be seen fishing. The best route through the gorge is simply to follow the low ruined wall to **Knack Mine Ford** $\textcircled{C}$ [SX614 884], although the last 100 meters or so are quite boggy so drift over to the right to avoid this wet part close to the ford and track.

Knack Mine Ford

As you reach the track coming down from the hillside on your right you will see the heaps of tinners' waste and a little further upstream are the ruins of **Knack Mine**, or Steeperton Mine as it was known when in operation.

Here is another opportunity to cut short your walk if you wish to by turning right up the hillside track to go back to Oke Tor on top of the hill and return to Belstone, thus making your walk about 7 miles.

After looking at the mine ruins our route takes us across the River Taw using the track to head towards **Hangingstone Hill** which is clearly visible ahead of you as a rounded hill with a building on its summit. The track you are following was once the main peat cutters' track from Belstone to Hangingstone. After climbing the hillside along the track the views to your left open up to **Wild Tor** across the other side of the **Steeperton Brook**, which has now appeared from the other side of Steeperton Tor.

The valley there can be quite boggy but there are a few tinners' ruins of interest to have a look at if you have time. Indeed, if you really don't want to follow the track then the west side of the Steeperton Brook is probably drier to walk on if you would rather walk across the moors. Whatever route you decide upon head up to the obvious hut at the summit of Hangingstone Hill $\textcircled{D}$, one of the major high points on the north moors with fine views all round.

To your west you have a fine view down into the head marshes of the **Taw River** as it rises from the boggy ground between you and **Cranmere Pool** [SX603 858]. Only a matter of 100 meters to the south are the head waters of the **East Dart River** which makes its way eventually to the English Channel at Dartmouth after an amazing journey.

To many, including me, this point epitomises the very centre of Devon where two of its greatest rivers are born, and where the splashing of Henry Williamson's otter, Tarka, can almost be heard as he heads north again along the Taw back to the North Devon coast, from his mammoth journey along the Torridge & the West Okement to Cranmere Pool. **The hut on Hangingstone Hill** is one of the military range lookout posts, out of bounds during live firing.

Hangingstone Hill gets its name from the odd-looking rock formation about 200 meters to the northwest where an overhanging stone is situated [SX615 864]. This rock is on our return journey and is fairly easy to locate on the hillside just tucked down out of sight of the top of the hill; there is a distinctively worn path leading to it.

After visiting the hanging stone our route takes us northwest down to the valley of the River Taw near to [SX609 865]. In this area look for the largest tinners' mound on the east bank of the river. The mound is about 30 feet high and huge for a spoil heap. At its summit is located the large memorial stone (E) to Ted Hughes, the Poet Laureate who died in 1998.

The Hanging Stone

From here our route is becoming well trodden by visitors to this point and leads us north west across the hillside parallel with the River Taw to the military range track leading from **OP15** [a large Observation Post structure] on the ring road [SX602 877]. Whether you choose to turn left on the track to OP15 or cross the track is up to you, but we eventually join the tarmac ring road and head in the direction of Oke Tor [SX612 900].

The road can be rather tiresome to walk along but is quicker than the adjoining heather clad moorland. There is a right hand junction to **Oke Tor,** which will lead you down to the Knack Mine track, but it is just as easy now that you can see Oke Tor ahead, to step out across the moors to it.

Once at Oke Tor (F) your views both left and right are magnificent. With the Summit of **Cosdon Beacon** now in view to the east and ahead of you through the valley of the Taw, the hills of Exmoor can be seen in the distance on a clear day. To your left are the impressive shapes of **Yes Tor** and **High Willhays** along with other rugged Tors including **West Mill** and **Row Tor.** Our route continues north along the ridge up to Higher Tor, past three boundary stones, and across the ruins of Irishman's Wall (G) to Belstone Tors.

Belstone Tor in the distance behind the boundary stones

From Belstone Tors it would be a shame to miss out on visiting the nearby **Nine Maidens Stone Circle** [SX613 928].

It is not immediately in view from the top of the tor but if you continue from the summit towards the flag pole on **Watchet Hill** your path is crossed by a grassy track leading from right to left. The easy way to find the stone circle is simply to turn left along this path, past the small quarry and you will find that the path leads to the stone circle. The circle actually has seventeen stones in it rather than nine, but the name probably refers to some pagan nature religion where nine had some significance.

Incidentally, the small quarry is of some interest because much of the stone there has been cut using the *'wedge and groove'* method, which was in use before the more common *'feather and tare'* adopted at the beginning of the 19th century.

Nine Maidens Stone Circle

Once you have visited the stone circle walk along the well-trod path to the north and you will join the larger vehicle track that leads to the moor gate by the **Belstone Water Treatment Works.** The lane will lead you back into the village, past the old **Telegraph Office** on your left and eventually to the start point in the village car park.

High Down Lydford to Bleak House & Sourton Ice Works

Length: Choice of a 5-mile walk or a 10-mile walk
Start: High Down Car Park, Dartmoor Inn, Lydford.
Grid ref: SX524 853
Difficulty: Moderate for both routes.

Blue route: 10-mile route; into the valley of the Doe Tor Brook and upstream to Dick's Well and onto Bleak House, then up to the Rattlebrook Peat Railway to Sourton Tors and the Ice Works then return via the Peat Railway to High Down. Red route: 5-mile deviation; by turning off early from Bleak House and returning to High Down over Great Links and Widgery Cross. This type of deviation can also be done on the railway line at 'Points' to suit whichever length of walk you desire.

1. High Down Lydford: SX524 85
2. Bleak House: SX559 864
3. Points: SX545 887
4. Ice Works: SX546 901
5. Great Nodden: SX539 874
6. Foot bridge: SX531 857

Some tracks as well as open moorland to cross. In poor visibility, especially on the section near Bleak House, a map and compass is essential. There are also a number of streams to cross, not all have bridges.

It is important to note that this walk follows beside the Wilsworthy Military Firing Range - it is essential to check the firing times and not to cross into the range past the red and white range posts when live firing is taking place. A Red flag is flown from nearby Doe Tor [SX541 848] when firing is occurring.

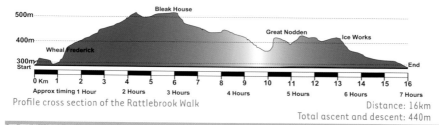

Profile cross section of the Rattlebrook Walk

Distance: 16km
Total ascent and descent: 440m

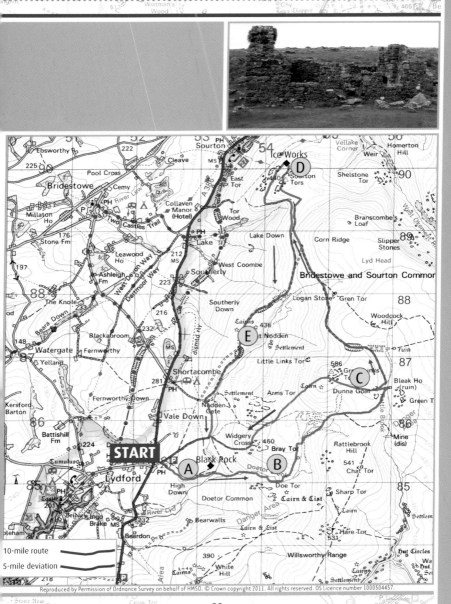

DARTMOOR wilderness walk 04

Park at the car park situated at High Down [SX524 853], which is located by taking the rough track beside the Dartmoor Inn, Lydford and through the gate at the top of the lane. Walk out onto the open moor by using the gate to the right when you are facing the moors. This way you go out onto the grassy downs following an obvious wide track which leads you to the ruins of **Wheal Mary Emma Mine** [SX530 852]. The higher mine workings now consist of a small indentation in the ground but a very obvious flat rod channel which leads down the hillside through the gorse.

The channel is a bit too overgrown to follow so use one of the clear paths to make your way down to the **River Lyd,** and the ruins of the mine workings beside the river near to the ford [SX532 851], just upstream from where **Doe Tor Brook** tumbles down the hillside into the Lyd.

Wheal Mary Emma Mine did not last long and few, if any, records of it survive. An interesting feature to see while you are here is the plaque on **Black Rock (A)** at [SX533 852] dedicated to the memory of Captain Nigel Hunter M.C [Bar] of the Royal Engineers who was killed near Bapaume on

Black Rock memorial

25th March 1918, aged 23 years. He wrote the poem now on his memorial on his last visit to Lydford, and after reading it you can't help but wonder if he knew that it would be his last trip to his beloved Dartmoor.

After leaving Black Rock walk back down the River Lyd to the ford by the mine workings and cross the river to walk up hill to join the left bank of the Doe Tor Brook. You do sometimes have to leave the bank of the brook to find suitable footing because it can get rather wet and steep here, but once you have passed by **Widgery Cross** on your left the land flattens out and you can easily follow the river as it bends left to the north. Alternatively there is an easy well trodden path which bends left over the gentle slope and follows along the course of the river to the ruins of **Wheal Frederick Mine (B)**, sometimes called *Foxhole Tin Mine.*

Wheal Frederick Mine ruins

The workings here are worthy of investigation. The old mine house is still in a surprisingly good condition. There is an impressive wheel-pit which has been filled in and also a pair of circular buddles below the ruins. After leaving Wheal Frederick cross the brook, there is a little bridge a short distance upstream, and walk upstream on the right hand bank because there is a very interesting Tinners' Cache beside the brook in the steep bank near to [SX549 858], thought to have been used to hide tin before being taken to one of the Stannary Towns to be assayed.

The best way to locate the cache is to walk near to the edge of the gully on your left and the gully turns to the right. Keep looking over the edge and you'll look right down into it. Once you have located and seen the cache go north across the stream to a large mound about 200 metres ahead on the uphill slope. This is the ruin of a reservoir used by the tinners to collect water. From here simply walk north again for about 100 metres and you reach the well-trodden pathway which was used by the peat cutters in the Rattlebrook valley.

At this point if you feel you would like to return to the start and your vehicles then simply turn left, westwards, and follow the distinctive path back to High Down ford and back to the car park.

If you are continuing on with the walk turn right, to the east, and follow the track to **Dick's Well** [SX551 861] where you will find a boundary stone marked with 'L' [Lydford] on one side and 'BS' [lands common to Bridestowe and Sourton] on the other. Continue east taking the left fork in the path to the River Rattlebrook and the ruins of **Bleak House** (C) [SX559 864] and the Rattlebrook Peat Works at the head of the Rattlebrook Railway.

The path swings left to the north to go below the small tor known as **Dunnagoat**. The best place to cross the Rattlebrook is just below Dunnagoat where there is a large stepping-stone in the stream. The peat works concentrated on the extraction of peat in the mid 19th Century but by the late 19th Century the venture had failed. It then continued spasmodically into the mid 20th Century and in 1961 the ruins were eventually blown up by the military.

Bleak House

Once visited, those who wish to only do the five-mile route need to either retrace their steps back past Dunnagoat to Dick's Well *(don't forget to fork right when the path splits)* and thence to **High Down Ford** along the distinctive path, or alternatively a more pleasant walk with fine views would be to go north west across the moors from Dunnagoat to Great Links Tor [SX550 867].

On a good day it is possible to see the sea on the north coast of Cornwall near Morewenstowe and on the south coast near Looe. Another possible visiting point on your journey home is the cross on **Brat Tor** [SX539 855].

This is known as **Widgery Cross** and was constructed at the behest of the Exeter painter, William Widgery, in 1887 in honour of Queen Victoria's Golden Jubilee. From here you make your way downhill to the High Down Ford and the track following the wall back to the car park.

Widgery Cross

For those leaving Bleak House with a view to doing the ten-mile route it is best to cross back to the west bank of the stream and to follow the distinctive footpath running on the high ground parallel to the river northwards to the railway line at the west end of the high embankment, which once carried the track across the mire and stream. If you follow the east bank the route is very boggy indeed as you near the ruins of the peat works [SX559 870]. Once on the old peat track you simply turn left into the cutting and follow the track across the hillside as it leads you to a sharp turn on the track called **'Points'** [SX545 887]. This is where there was a turn about for the trucks because of the steep incline and change in direction.

If you wish to cut your walk short at this stage you simply follow the track downhill and over **Great Nodden** [SX538 874] to Nodden Gate, then simply follow the River Lyd, using the east bank, downstream to High Down Ford and along the track back to the car park. **For those wishing to continue their route all the way to the Ice Works** go along the track into the turn-about area and carry on northwards along a well-trodden path towards **Sourton Tors** ahead of you [SX453 898]. The Tors are initially out of sight but soon appear around the corner when you walk along the path.

It is easier to walk to the right of the tors and go to the north at a point near [SX545 901] where you will locate the longs ridges and ruins of the Ice Works **D** just over the hillcrest. Ice was produced here at the latter end of the 19th Century because of the altitude and conditions, as well as the close proximity of the railway to take ice to Plymouth where it was used in the fish markets and the Barbican. Indeed there was an intention to take a branch from the Rattlebrook Railway to the Ice Works but this never came about. Unfortunately the venture failed shortly after it started and the workings were abandoned.

Cider Press base

Another interesting feature in this area is an abandoned cider press base, which is located east of Sourton Tors on the grassy plain at the foot of the slop between Sourton Tors and the steep slop leading up to Branscombe's Loaf.

Once you have looked at the ruins and the crusher your return journey is best to retrace your tracks back to 'Points' on the railway track and then follow the track, as already described back downhill and over Great Nodden to the River Lyd, and down the Lyd to High Down ford and back to the car park.

A brief, but interesting diversion, on the very summit of **Great Nodden** **E** is an interesting cairn.

The Ice Works ruins and Sourton Tor

Stall Down and the Erme Valley

Length: Choice of a 5-mile walk or a 10-mile walk
Start: Harford Moor Gate Car Park, 3km North of Ivybridge
Grid ref: SX643 595
Difficulty: Moderate for both. The 5-mile route involves one steep section, the 10-mile route involves an hour of long grass.

Blue route: 10-miles; through the newly defined CROW Act land and into the valley of the River Erme and upstream to Erme Pound then across to the east of the river to the disused Red Lake Railway track. Then return south along the track to Spurrell's Cross and west back to the car park at Harford Moor Gate.

Red route: 5-mile deviation; by turning off early to cross the Erme just north of Piles Copse and then make for the Red Lake Railway track then continue to Spurrell's Cross and the car park.

Both of these routes lie outside of the firing ranges so can be undertaken at any time of the year. However, a crossing of the River Erme is necessary on either route and therefore it is recommended to only undertake the walk when the river is low and easier to ford.

1. Harford Moor Gate: SX643 595
2. Tristis Rock:
3. Downings House: SX638 601
4. Erme Pound: SX638 629
5. Three Barrows: SX637 656
6. Spurrell's Cross: SX653 625
   SX658 599

Grid

The 10-mile route takes in some of the most remote parts of southern Dartmoor so is not to be undertaken lightly or without the proper clothing and equipment.

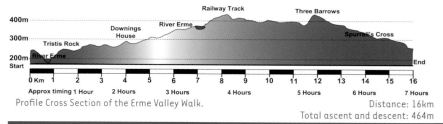

Profile Cross Section of the Erme Valley Walk.

Distance: 16km
Total ascent and descent: 464m

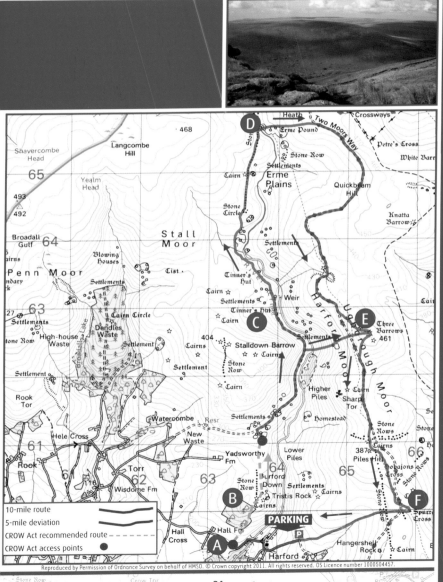

Despite there being lots of features on this walk, in both good as well as in poor visibility, a map and compass are **essential** especially on the 10-mile section north of the Water Company's Dam and in the area of Erme Pound.

Park at the car park at Harford Moor Gate [SX643 595], where there is a gate and plenty of parking available. **Ensure that no valuables are left in your vehicle** and as always, leave details of your route and estimated time of return with someone. Be aware that much of this route is out of signal for many of the mobile phone services, especially in the deep valley of the River Erme.

Gateway at Harford

From the car park walk back through the gate down to **Harford Church** continuing downhill to Harford Bridge. Go over the bridge and continue around the left bend; go uphill passing Harford Bridge Cottage on your left. [Don't go through the first gate on your right, the sign warning about a bull being loose will put off most walkers!] Carry on up the hill passing a **conveniently painted white stone** on your left until you go around a right hand bend to find a second gate on your right. (A) This gate is marked as **'Permissive Path'**. Go through this gate and follow the well-defined footpath, which goes up the hillside. You will pass by a few new CROW Act signs as you go along the well defined path through walls and eventually out onto the open moor through a gate at the corner of **Hall Plantation** [SX636 600].

Continue towards **Tristis Rock** [SX638 601], which you can see ahead of you. Over to your right, to the east, you have fine views over the opposite hillside, which you will be walking back over on your return journey.
If you would like to visit a nearby kistaven simply walk about 50 metres west of **Tristis Rock** (B) to the first gorse bush, where you will locate it hidden in the gorse.

Tristis Rock

From Tristis Rock our path is well defined and heads north through a prehistoric settlement and eventually goes through a gate with a CROW Act sign in the wall. Pass through this gate and continue north for about 500 metres towards the final wall with a wire fence on top. The footpath leads you toward the right slightly but if you lose the path, simply carry on towards the wall and turn right to locate the final pedestrian gateway out onto the open moorland [SX639 610].

Go through the gate and out onto the open moors, going uphill in a north-westerly direction until you reach the rough Water Company vehicle track which goes through quite an impressive settlement with hut circles all around you.

When you reach the track simply turn right and follow it into the valley of the River Erme. As you walk along you will see **Piles Copse Woods** on your right [SX643 621] on the other side of the river. This is one of the three ancient oak woods on Dartmoor, the other

Piles Copse woods

two being the **Wistman's Wood** near Two Bridges and **Black-a-Tor Copse** in the valley of the West Okement near Okehampton on the north moors.

High above Piles Copse is Sharp Tor. There is a well-defined wall going all the way around Piles Copse. When you reach a point at the end of the Piles Copse enclosure it is here that the five-mile deviation leaves the track.

For those wishing to do the 5-mile route you simply walk down diagonally to the right just as the track reaches a lone Hawthorn tree on your left. Go down to the river to where the enclosure wall comes down the hillside on the other side.

There are a few places here to cross the river; don't go any further upstream because the ground on the other side of the river is boggy.

Once you have crossed the river simply walk up the steep hill with the wall on your right, when the wall bends to the right just carry on eastward until you reach the **Red Lake Railway track**. You then follow the 10-mile route back to the car park.

For those carrying on with the longer route, continue along the track to a gully on your left [SX638 629] where the small Downing Brook runs down the hillside. If you take a little deviation of a few metres you will locate **Downing's House** , a small tinner's beehive shelter where tools and ingots could have been hidden, for it is too small to be a proper shelter for a man. To find it simply walk up the brook towards the tree ahead of you, stay on the right bank and about halfway between the track and the tree you will stumble across the small ruin.

Downing's House

After looking at Downing's House, simply carry on up the track to the Water Company hut and dam [SX639 631] where the track ends at the head of the Water Works on the River Erme. Pass by the hut and you will find a footpath going northwards up the valley. Looking over to the right you will notice two streams coming down the hillside. One is the **Left Lake** and the other is the **Dry Lake.**

For those wanting to cut the 10-mile route a little shorter, perhaps due to time, it is possible to cross the Erme here [SX640 663] and walk up the first of these brooks to the railway track [SX646 634] where the 10-mile route rejoins you. All around you are now the familiar herringbone patterns of the tinners' waste heaps beside the river.

The River Erme now goes either side of an island [SX637 635] and our path goes left slightly into the valley of a small brook running down from our left. Cross the brook and continue up the Erme valley. When you look to the right over to the other side of the Erme you will see a few very distinct settlement enclosures.

Looking ahead upstream in the direction that we are travelling you can see on the left hill that there is a brighter green enclosure [SX635 642] higher up above the Erme.

We are going to be heading for that greener enclosure once we have negotiated the boggy area ahead of us caused by the draining **Blatchford Brook** coming down from our left. Simply follow the brook upstream to the left to the first tree where there is a pool and a large number of boulders below the pool where you can easily cross the brook.

Make your way across the low wet area and start going up the hillside on the other side of the small brook. As you go uphill the ground is quite difficult because of the length of the grass and being quite wet but this soon ends as you gain the rise. There are a few paths to pick up which lead to the greener enclosure area, where you will find some hut circles. We now continue uphill to the stone circle [SX635 644] known as **Kiss-in-the-Ring** and the start of the longest stone row on Dartmoor, and allegedly, in the world.

Our route now simply follows the stone row and the distinct path that runs beside it all the way to the River Erme. We pass a large cairn on the way, itself worth a brief detour to inspect. As the stone row drops down to cross the River Erme we part company with it to go to the remains of **Erme Pound** **D** [SX637 656], a Bronze Age enclosure that has several huts within it. It was later used as an animal pound. The River Erme is easily crossed in this area to reach the Pound. Once visited, the route simply goes due east to join the Red Lake Trackway [SX644 657]. At the track turn right and start walking on your return journey southwards.

Erme Pound

After about 500 metres you pass by the brick built mica-settling pits on your left [SX649 656]. These were used in the clay industry of this area and well worth a brief deviation to have a look at. Once back on the track you simply follow it for 6 kilometres to **Spurrell's Cross.** [SX658 599]

On the way along the track you pass by the old clay pit at **Left Lake** [SX647 634] and then on your left you will see the high **Three Barrows** **E** [SX653 625] - well worth a closer look at. There is also a distinct Reeve [a prehistory land boundary] running through this location marked on the map.

Cairns on Three Barrows

You next pass **Sharp Tor** on your right [SX647 617] with views across the Erme valley over to Stalldown and Hillson's House.

There are a number of crosses, which a small deviation will allow you to visit. One being **Hobajon's Cross** [SX655 604] and finally **Spurrell's Cross** **F** which isn't actually on the former railway track but about 100 metres east of it.

It is at this point that there is a distinct grassy path leading west across the hillside and downhill to the car park at Harford Moor Gate and your car.

Spurrell's Cross looking over the south Devon countryside

The Erme Valley

DARTMOOR
wilderness walk 06

Yes Tor and Cranmere Pool

Length: Choice of a 5-mile walk or a 10-mile walk
Start: Parking area at 'Okehampton Moor' where the military ring road splits.
Grid ref: SX596 922
Difficulty: Arduous climbing starts to both routes with easy returns along a track.

Blue route: 10-mile route; over Row Tor [SX593 916] and West Mill Tor [SX587 909] up to Yes Tor [SX580 902] and on to High Willhays [SX580 894] before dropping to Dinger Tor [SX586 881] and onto Cranmere Pool [SX602 858]. Return via Ted Hughes' memorial [SX609 864] in the Taw valley and the east side of the military ring road. Red route: 5-mile deviation; by turning off early at Dinger Tor and returning along the military track northwards back to the car park taking in the Target Railway [SX593 910] remains on the way.

Some rough tracks as well as open moorland to cross. In poor visibility, especially on the **Cranmere Pool s**ection of this walk, a map and compass is essential. There are also a number of streams and bogs to cross on the 10-mile route.

It is important to note that this walk enters the Okehampton Military Firing Range - it is essential to check the firing times and not to undertake this walk when live firing is taking place on the Okehampton Firing Range. Equally the 10-mile route crosses some of the most difficult terrain that Dartmoor has to offer. The ground is invariably very wet at most times of the year so expect wet feet!

1. Okehampton Moor: SX596 92
2. Yes Tor: Grid SX580 902
3. Dinger Tor: SX586 881
4. Cranmere Pool: SX602 858
5. OP15: SX602 877
6. Target Railway: SX593 910

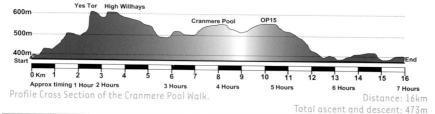

Profile Cross Section of the Cranmere Pool Walk.

Approx timing 1 Hour 2 Hours 3 Hours 4 Hours 5 Hours 6 Hours 7 Hours

Distance: 16km
Total ascent and descent: 473m

41

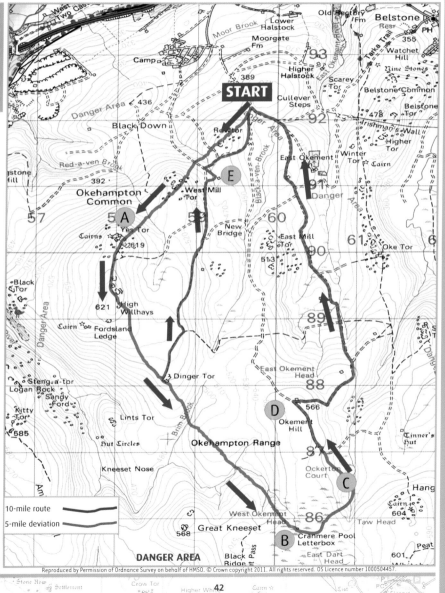

START

A

B

C

D

E

10-mile route

5-mile deviation

Leave your car at the parking area [SX596 922] where there are the barriers, which drop down to block the tracks when firing is taking place. This is where the military ring road splits. From here walk south west to the nearby **Row Tor** [SX593 916] and then onto **West Mill** [SX587 909] with its avenue of rocks on the summit of the tor. From here you have a good view down and up to the impressive **Yes Tor** [SX580 902] high above you.

From **West Mill Tor** up to **Yes Tor** it is barely a kilometre but it is rather a long slog with a rather small bog [SX584 904] at the foot of the hill as you cross the small stream. It isn't difficult to pick your way through it in wet conditions.

Yes Tor

Once you arrive at the summit of Yes Tor (A) [SX580 902] at over 2,000 feet above sea level the views make the effort worthwhile. On a clear day the whole of North Devon is laid out before you with glimpses of the sea near Bude on the North Cornwall coast. Yes Tor is the highest actual Tor on Dartmoor although High Willhays is marginally higher but not strictly speaking a Tor.

The track from Yes Tor to High Willhays [SX580 894] is an easy one to follow as it heads south; giving the false impression that High Willhays is lower in altitude. There are a number of outcrops at High Willhays but the one to take your triumphant photograph at is the outcrop with the cairn perched on top. From here you have a fine view of the higher tors of the North Moor with a 360° panorama and a spectacular vista over the West Okement valley below you to the west. The route continues south and east as it bends slightly to the left going downhill over the heather covered slopes, following a track to **Dinger Tor** [SX586 881], with its military vehicle turning area next to the tor itself.

It is here that the 10-mile and 5-mile routes part. If you wish to return to the cars along the 5-mile route at this point you simply head northwards along the military track, passing High Willhays and Yes Tor high above you.

Once you reach **West Mill Tor** on your left look over to the right across the grass to the small building which houses the restored military target railway engine [SX593 910]. There is also the target railway line leading in a loop from the shed and back again - a relic of a bygone military age, painstakingly restored and preserved by enthusiasts.

The route then simply heads north towards Row Tor. When you come across the military track again where you turn right and follow it back to your car at the barriers, and junction of the military ring road. **For those continuing with the 10-mile route from Dinger Tor,** you head south east to cross the stream at the ruins of a substantial tinner's hut [SX590 877]. The ground here can be a bit wet but not difficult to cross.

Continue up the rising ground ahead of you to the south-east and drop to cross the stream of Vergyland Combe [SX595 869]. Follow the stream downhill to where there is another stream joining it from the left [SX595 867] an easy way to locate the often elusive Cranmere Pool [SX602 858] is to simply follow the stream, sticking on the left bank, all the way up to the large depression where Cranmere Pool **B** letter box is located. There is a well trodden path in the grass to follow as you go higher up the stream, especially as you pass the access points to the stream from Okerton Court over to your left from where people often approach Cranmere Pool.

Cranmere Pool letter box

The letterbox at the pool has been here in various forms since a Dartmoor guide who brought ramblers to this remote place established it over a century ago.

After a well-earned rest at the letterbox your route now takes you easterly towards **Hangingstone Hill** [SX617 861]. You can see the hill in clear weather with its distinctive square hut on the summit. Walk over the peat hags towards the Hangingstone direction, crossing some really wet and boggy ground as you approach the headwaters of the **Rivers Taw** and **East Dart.**

As the ground starts to drop away from you left and right into the river valleys you are at a point, which many feel, is the centre of Devon. 100 metres to your left is the River Taw, which eventually flows out through Barnstaple on the North Devon coast, whereas on your right you are looking down the River [East] Dart, which eventually flows out to the sea at Dartmouth on the south coast.

Turn to the north and leftwards and follow the taw valley with the young stream on your right. The valley soon opens out and evidence of significant tinworks and 'streaming' exist. Ahead of you and down in the river valley [SX609 864] is a solitary and very large tinner's mound the size of a house. On the summit of this mount is a large granite slab carved with the name of **Ted Hughes,** a former Poet Laureate and acquaintance of the Prince of Wales who granted permission for this monument. **C** .

From here continue northwards along a path, which frequent visitors to the monument are unwittingly establishing, and which leads you across the moor to join the military vehicle track. Turn left along the track and follow it to **OP 15 D** , [SX602 877] one of the military observations posts situated on the junction when you reach the military ring road.

OP 15

You might find a few vehicles parked next to the building, left by motorists who are prepared to brave the rugged state of the ring road! The building affords splendid shelter in bad weather and is maintained by the military especially for that purpose as a useful shelter in such a remote spot.

The return journey back to your car will be along the ring road, in itself an easy route to follow but also affording some lovely views of the north moor while being able to maintain a reasonable pace. Whether you turn to the right and return to your car via the east route or turn left to follow the westerly route is entirely up to you.

The distance is the same and takes just a bit over an hour at a brisk stroll. If you wish to take a look at the Target Railway [SX593 910] **E** then choose the left, westerly, route and you can make a small detour across the grass to view the complex before reaching your car.

High Willhays

North Moor Wilderness

Length: Choice of a 5-mile walk or a 10-mile walk
Start: Car Park at Baggator Gate Lane End, Wilsworthy.
Grid ref: SX546 805
Difficulty: Moderate for the 5-mile route and arduous on the
10-mile route due to long sections of long grass.

Blue route: Just short of 10-miles; Up towards Lynch Tor and follow the peat cutters' track to the River Tavy. Then up to Fur Tor and east to Cut Hill. Return via the source of the River Tavy to Lynch Tor and back to Baggator Gate. Red route: 5-mile deviation; by turning off early at the River Tavy and by following it south to where the 10-mile route crosses it from the east. Then return to Baggator Gate along the 10-mile return route. Both of these routes lie within the Merrivale and Okehampton firing ranges so can only be undertaken on days when there is no live firing on those military ranges. Details of the firing times and days of firing can be obtained on the Internet at www.dartmoor-ranges. co.uk [and simply click on 'firing notice'] or alternatively by phone on **0800 4584868.**

1. Baggator Gate: SX546 80
2. Tavy Hole: SX580 819
3. Fur Tor: SX587 831
4. Cut Hill: SX598 827
5. South Tavy Head: SX595 819
6. Lynch Tor: SX565 807

Grid

The 10-mile route takes in some of the remotest parts of Dartmoor so is not to be undertaken lightly or without the proper clothing and equipment. Despite there being lots of features on this walk, in both good as well as in poor visibility a map and compass are essential especially on the 10-mile section east of Lynch Tor.

Profile Cross Section of the North Moor Wilderness Walk.

Distance: 16km
Total ascent and descent: 417m

North Moor Wilderness

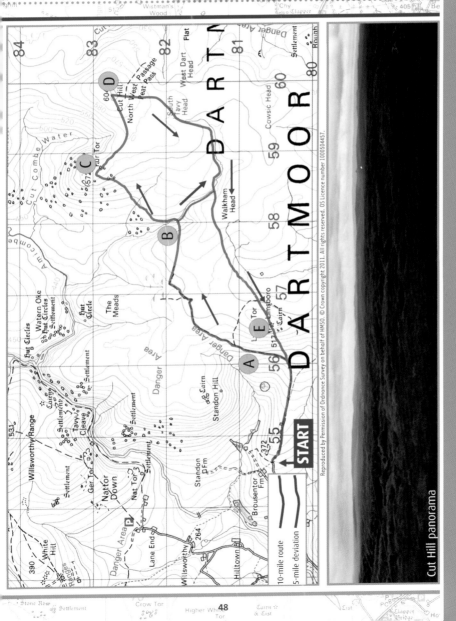

Cut Hill panorama

10-mile route

5-mile deviation

START

48

It will also be necessary to cross the River Tavy as well as a number of its tributaries on the 10-mile route. Therefore it is advisable only to undertake this route when the rivers are low. **The 10-mile route is one of the most arduous** in these series due to the difficult terrain. It is for that reason that it has been left at just short of the usual 10-miles, but will take just as long to complete. The 5-mile route doesn't involve any river crossings.

Park at the car park at Baggator Gate 4 km Northeast of Peter Tavy [SX620 536]. There is enough parking for about 4 cars at the gate. **Do ensure you do not block any of the farm tracks leading in various directions from here. Nearby there is the Firing Range hut at the gateway onto the moors** [SX551 803] where there is a range notice board and a member of range staff when live firing is taking place. Ensure that no valuables are left in your vehicle and, as always, leave details of your route and estimated time of return with someone. Be aware that much of this route is out of signal for many of the mobile phone services, especially in the Tavy valley.

From your car walk along the main rough stony track to the range hut [SX551 803]. This rough track follows the line of the ancient **Lych Way** from **Bellever** to **Lydford Church,**
used for the carriage of bodies for burial from the moorland parishes. Go through the gateway by the range hut and out onto the open moors along the tapering drift lane used for bringing livestock off the moors in times gone by. In the middle of the drift lane there is a noticeable footpath following a deep gully. It begins to swing to the left as you approach **Lynch Tor** [SX565 807] high up ahead of you and instead of climbing the slopes of Lynch Tor you simply follow this peat cutters' pathway (A) as it crosses the moors northwards across the slopes of Lynch Tor.

Lynch Tor

The path is quite deep and very distinct as it climbs gently up and to the north of Lynch Tor. You will see ahead and to the left of you, a line of red and white posts marking the boundary of the Wilsworthy Firing Range. **Be sure not to venture across this line of poles if there is firing on that range.** Your path then contours around the hill leading out onto the open moors.

The start of the River Tavy

There are a few cairns marking the route of the track until it doubles back on itself. In the distance to the north-east you will see **Fur Tor** [SX587 831] far away in the centre of the north moor. This is the destination of the 10-mile route.

If you look to the right of Fur Tor you will see a flagpole about a kilometre away; head for the flagpole [SX576 819]. The ground can by a bit wet in this location and the grass is quite long. Once you reach the flag pole start heading slightly to the right of Fur Tor and drop into the valley of the River Tavy at Tavy Hole **B** [SX580 819].

When you drop down you will lose sight of Fur Tor so if you are doing the 10-mile route make a mental note of which is the most accurate way up the hillside once you have crossed the stream of the River Tavy. Down by the river there are some pretty waterfalls [SX580 818] and a good site for a picnic. **This is where those on the 5-mile route leave the main route** and head upstream to the right and follow the banks of the Tavy for about a kilometre to a point [SX585 812] where the 10-mile route crosses the river on its return from Fur Tor. Once the 5-mile route reaches this point it simply follows the return journey of the 10-mile route.

River Tavy at Tavy Hole

If you are following the main 10-mile walk you simply cross the Tavy at one of the many fording spots with large boulders and climb the hillside ahead of you until you get a view again of Fur Tor. It's best to aim to the right of Fur Tor in the distance because of the wet ground ahead and to the left of you as you contour around the **Fur Tor Brook** [SX583 823]. **You are now approaching the most remote of Dartmoor Tors** with a wonderful sense of isolation. As you approach the main outcrop **C** of the tor take a few minutes to locate the letterbox hidden in the large cleft in the tor [SX587 830]. The views from here are spectacular to the north but are certainly surpassed by the views of **Cut Hill** [SX598 827], which you can see over to the east on the other side of Fur Tor.

You might feel isolated at Fur Tor but Cut Hill is the most remote spot on Dartmoor and will take another half an hour to reach. The route to Cut Hill basically contours around the hillside with a slope off to your left. The terrain is tortuous and covered in peat cuttings and numerous bogs, which you have to zigzag to get through. The sense of achievement upon reaching Cut Hill **D** is certainly worth the effort and if you walk up to the very top of the hill and stand aloft the highest of the peat hags you will achieve what must be one of the best views on the moors.

Dartmoor is spread out before you through 360°. On a fine day you can see the clay tips of St Austell down in Cornwall to the west and towards the east you might glimpse Portland Bill in Dorset! But the nearby tors of the moor are set out in all directions. To the north you have **High Willhays,** the highest point in southern England, to the south views as far at Ryder's Hill and Three Barrows on the south moor can be enjoyed in clear weather. In the huge depression of Cut Hill there are a number of flat stones, the one in the middle of the depression is faintly carved with the word "JEW" and is knows as the 'Jew Stone'. Nobody quite knows why it bears this inscription.

Once you have finished at Cut Hill head south towards the start of the Peat Cutting known as the **North West Passage.** This is a granite post [SX597 825] with a bronze plaque on it with an inscription about the crossing being made by Frank Phillpotts, for the use of hunting and cattlemen to cross the moors.

The Jew Stone

From here the route really becomes very arduous with long grass, and wet underfoot. We now head south to the headwaters of the River Tavy. You can see the route clearly as it drops down into the top of the valley ahead of you and slips down into the depression ahead [SX595 819]. Drop down into the start of the valley to locate the spring from which the Tavy flows, it is easier to cross the valley and walk down following parallel to the Tavy on your left. There are a few narrow sheep tracks here, which might be of some help in negotiating the long grass.

The route follows down the valley and around a right bend where there is a tinner's hut [SX593 814] marked on the map but very difficult to locate. **A second hut** [SX589 813] is also marked on the map but equally difficult to find.

Philpotts' Peat Pass marker stone

The river turns to the right; up ahead of you in the distance is the hill leading up to Lynch Tor. It is this hill that you are aiming for as you continue down the river. Looking to your left you will see a stream coming down from the left from the **South Tavy Head** [SX588 811]. After the junction of this small tributary you walk ahead and cross the Tavy. Don't continue around to the right too far or you will simply drop downhill, losing valuable height.

Cross the Tavy through the deep rushes. *There is a good marker to look out for and this is a sandy bank on the other side of the river.* Head for the sandy bank [SX586 812] and there are some useful boulders for crossing the stream here. This is where the 5-mile route has come up the stream to join us from Tavy Hole. You will have lost the view of Lynch Tor but simply carry on heading for the top of the hill and over the crest to regain the view in the distant west towards Lynch Tor. As you cross the deep grass you find a few paths that are very welcome after the difficulties of the long vegetation.

Make towards the right of Lynch Tor, a small outcrop on the hillside ahead of you with a flagpole on top. This is actually the cairn on the top of the hill as the true tor itself is just over the ridge. As you head to the right of the flagpole and cairn you will begin to see a granite post [SX586 805] at the foot of the slope leading up to Lynch Tor. Aim for that post and then up to the cairn and nearby tor **E**.

The views to the west open up again and Fur Tor behind you seems a very long way away, and your legs no doubt will be telling the tale too! Visit the nearby Tor [SX564 807] and then drop down into the drift lane which leads you back onto the peat cutter's track and to the gate at Baggator range hut.

A short walk leads you to your vehicle. The nearby **Baggator** outcrop [SX547 805] affords some lovely views down into the valley beyond and is worth a small diversion at the end of the walk. I am sure that those who have bravely completed the longer route will agree that it did seem significantly further than 10-miles!

Rough Tor and the West Dart valley

Length: Choice of a 5-mile walk or a 10-mile walk
Start: Car park at the Two Bridges
Grid ref: SX609 750
Difficulty: Easy going for the 5-mile route with paths and tracks. Moderate for the 10-mile route due to the remoteness.

Blue route: 10-mile route; from Two Bridges - north along the track past Crockern Cottage [SX609 756] and up to Wistmans Wood [SX612 770]. Then northeast over Longaford [SX615 778] Tor to Higher White Tor [SX619 785]. Continuing northwest to Brown's House [SX614 798] and westerly to Rough Tor [SX606 798] and Devils Tor [SX596 796] into Conies Down Water [SX591 793], before heading back easterly to Lydford Tor [SX599 781] and down to the Devonport Le[SX608 779]. Follow the Devonport leat back to Beardown Farm [SX604 754] and Two Bridges.

Red route: 5-mile deviation; after leaving Wistmans Wood simply follow the West Dart valley upstream to the leat take-off weir [SX608 779] and cross over onto the east side and follow the 10-mile route down the Devonport Leat.

1. Two Bridges Car park: SX609 75
2. Wistmans Wood: SX612 77;
3. Longaford Tor: SX615 779
4. Browns House: SX614 798
5. Beardown Man: SX596 796
6. Devonport Leat: SX608 779

Some rough tracks as well as open moorland to cross. In poor visibility, especially on the section of this walk after **Wistmans Wood,** a map and compass are essential. There are also a number of streams and bogs to cross on the 10-mile route.

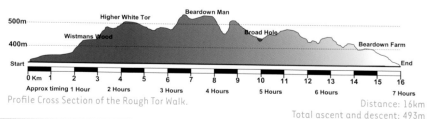

Profile Cross Section of the Rough Tor Walk.

Distance: 16km
Total ascent and descent: 493m

53

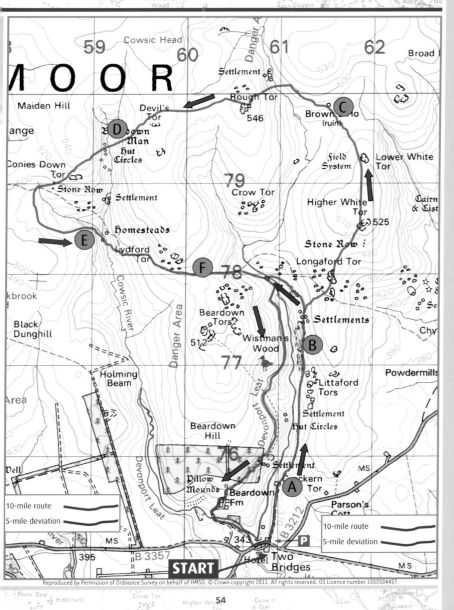

It is important to note that this walk enters the Merrivale Military Firing Range - it is essential to check the firing times and not to undertake this walk when live firing is taking place on the Merrivale Firing Range. Firing information can be obtained from: www.dartmoor-ranges.co.uk or telephone 0800 4584868 It may also be broadcast on BBC Radio Devon.

Equally the 10-mile route crosses some of the most difficult terrain that Dartmoor has to offer. The ground is invariably very wet at most times of the year so expect wet feet! On the 5-mile route a crossing of the weir is necessary so it is best to avoid a time when the right is high, alternatively just downstream of the weir there are a number of places to cross the West Dart on the boulders.

Leave your car at the parking area [SX609 750] on the opposite side of the road from the Two Bridges Hotel in the old quarry car park. From your car walk north and through the five bar gate along the rough vehicle track to Crockern Cottage [SX609 756]. Pass the cottage on your left using the well-worn footpath that leads all the way to Wistman's Wood [SX612 770] through the fields. On the way you will pass by a few well-preserved rabbit burrows [SX611 758], also known as 'Pillow Mounds' (A). These were man-made rabbit warrens where the Warrener used to keep rabbits commercially for their meat.

Buller Stone

There was a warren house at the far end of Wistman's Wood in the last century. The footpath is easily followed as it makes its way to the ancient oak wood of Wistman's Wood. One interesting feature here is a large triangular rock known as the **'Buller Stone'** (B) [SX612 774] upon which is carved the following: *"By permission of H. R. H. the Prince of Wales, Wentworth Buller, on September 16th 1866, cut down a tree near this spot; it measured nine inches in diameter, and appeared to be about one hundred and sixty-eight years old"*. It is located just off the track and in the edge of the wood as you follow the path around the top of the wood. Once you have passed the wood the grassy platform of the warren house can be located to the north of the wood [SX612 775].

It is here where the 5-mile route and 10-mile routes deviate. The 5-mile route simply follows the West Dart River upstream to the weir [SX608 779] where you can cross onto the west bank. Once on the west bank simply follow the 10-mile route as it returns down the **Devonport Leat,** mentioned later. If the crossing at the weir looks a little too ambitious for you then walk downstream about 50 metres to an alternative crossing point by some large boulders.

The 10-mile route, however, now climbs to Longaford Tor [SX615 778] to enjoy some far-reaching views over to the south and west. You can also see over and into the valley of the East Dart River north of Postbridge. From here our route follows a fairly well defined path through the long grass to **Higher White Tor** [SX619 785]. There is a rather indistinct stone row [SX619 783] to be found on the way to Higher White Tor just to the right of the path [if the grass is not too long]. Once at Higher White Tor [SX619 785] the views open up to the east far away to Hameldown

Brown's House ruins

and southeast towards Hay Tor. From this tor we head north over the stile to the smaller Lower White Tor [SX619 792] almost due north of us.

Looking northwest you will see the low ruins of Brown's House [SX614 798] on the other side of a boggy section of lower ground. Between Lower White Tor and Brown's House is a distinct ruin of a tinner's building [SX615 797]. If you visit this ruin on the way to Brown's House you will be following about the best route for keeping your feet dry! At **Brown's House** Ⓒ you will find a few low walls but not much of a ruinous building. Legend has it that the farm was constructed by a jealous Mr Brown who hid his beautiful wife there, away from the gaze of other admiring men!

Continue northeast into the valley of the West Dart, which you can cross where the ruined wall passes over the stream [SX610 800]. Follow the wall ruins uphill westerly and up to **Rough Tor** [SX606 798].

From Rough Tor [the highest point of the walk] there are good views to the north towards Cut Hill and the desolate areas of the north moor. From here our route goes across quite a wet area to **Devil's Tor** [SX596 796], which is a very small, remote and indistinct outcrop on the horizon. There are a few paths leading across this rather bleak area and it's best to follow one of these. Once you reach the low lying and small Devil's Tor you will find the large and isolated standing stone - **'Beardown Man'**  [SX596 796] - on the western flank of Devil's Tor. The view here to the west opens up as well as good views down the **Cowsick River** towards **Princetown** and **North Hessary Mast** [a good navigational aid] as well as Fur Tor to the north on a clear day.

Rough Tor

Conies Down Tor [SX589 791] lies to our southwest on the other side of the Cowsick and it is best to simply head straight for it and down into the valley. There is a good ford [SX591 793] on the direct line but if you try to contour around the valley it gets very boggy. Skirt around the hillside and past Conies Down Tor to the west. There is another very difficult-to-locate stone row [SX585 790] with just a few small and low stones to indicate its presence here. The route crosses the little stream known as **Conies Down Water** and contours up a track from a ford [SX587 786], uphill to two triangular rocks on the hillside. In the higher of the two rocks [SX590 785] is a small cleft where there is

Traveller's Ford Cross

hidden a small bronze memorial cross, **Traveller's Ford Cross,** inside the rock, surrounded by quartz crystals, almost forming a small grotto  . [The cross was missing at time of print].

From the bronze cross rock the route drops down to the distinct ford at **Broad Hole** [SX591 786], also known as *Traveller's Ford* on the **Lych Way,** also known as **'The Way of the Dead'** - used for carrying bodies for burial at Lydford Church in mediaeval times. We cross the Cowsick here again and follow the distinct track easterly uphill to Lydford Tor [SX599 781] through the gateway.

As the route passes by Lydford Tor start looking to the right of the path. As you crest the hill and start to drop downhill look out for a well-hidden **Cist** [SX603 780] (F) on the right of the track in the long grass. It is really difficult to find but is it a good example and worth hunting for!

Beardown Man

The path now goes downhill and drops into the West Dart valley to the take off weir for the **Devonport Leat** [SX608 779]. Our return journey follows the leat path downstream for about two kilometres all the way into the woods at **Beardown plantation** [SX608 759]. Walk along the leat and through the woods until the leat reaches the vehicle track [SX604 756] coming up from **Beardown Farm** down to our left. We turn left on the track and down towards the farm and turn right through a gate [SX604 755] just before you reach the farm buildings. The road takes you right and around the edge of the farm enclosures and right again downhill.

As you reach the bottom of the hill there is a gate on the right [SX602 753]. If you go through the gate you will find a well-preserved **clapper bridge** [SX602 753] crossing the Cowsick River and this is well worth a small diversion to go and see. This bridge is one of the two bridges that gave its name to the nearby community of **Two Bridges.** The other clapper bridge over the West Dart near Crockern Cottage has long since been swept away or demolished.

Our route now returns back through the gate to the main vehicle track and down to the road bridge [SX603 753] over the Cowsick River. Once over the bridge, drop down left onto the footpath [SX603 752] marked by a finger post. **Just by the bridge there are a few boulders which have been inscribed with the names of poets,** one is the big flat stone just below the road level.

We now follow the marked footpath into the enclosure of the woods over the stile [SX606 750].The path takes us through the woods and the field into a narrow laneway over a further stile. This lane leads us out onto the main road by **Two Bridges** [SX607 749], where we turn left to return to our car at the quarry car park [SX609 750].

Venford and Ryder's Hill

Length: Choice of a 5-mile walk or a 10-mile walk
Start: Car Park at the western end of Venford Reservoir, with facilities and a local tourist information notice board.
Grid ref: SX685 712
Difficulty: Moderate for both routes.

Blue route: 10-miles; Southwest Horn's Cross and Hooten Wheals mine ruins, the west to Skir Gut and up to Ryder's Hill before heading southwards towards Huntingdon Warren. Return north via Pupers Hill and Snowdon then via Hapstead Ford to Venford. **Red route: 5-mile deviation;** by turning off early in the gully leading up from the O Brook and turning left following the line of boundary stones up to Ryder's Hill. Once at Ryder's Hill you then turn left and eastwards to Hapstead Ford and join the return route of the 10-mile walk.
Both of these routes lie outside of the firing ranges so can be undertaken at any time of the year.

1. Venford Reservoir: SX685 71
2. Skir Gut: SX647 70
3. Ryder's Hill: SX659 690
4. Clapper Bridge: SX657 661
5. Pupers Hill: SX672 673
6. Snowdon: SX668 682

However, a crossing of a number of small rivers is necessary on the 10-mile route. Some of these can rise quite quickly in wet weather so check the forecast before undertaking the 10-mile section. The routes also cross quite arduous ground sometimes in quite deep grass, which can be tiring. There are also a few steep climbs, so quite an ambitious walk.

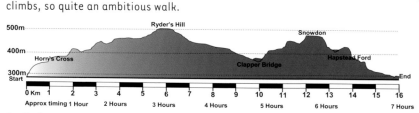

Profile Cross Section of the Venford Walk.

Distance: 16km
Total ascent and descent: 456m

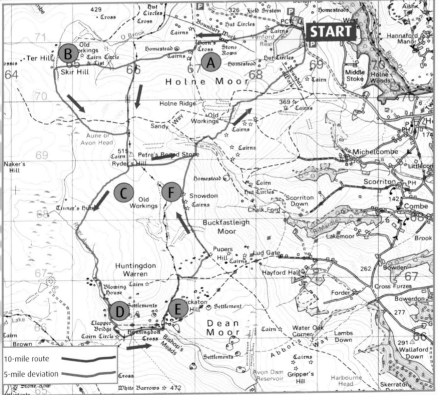

10-mile route

5-mile deviation

Both routes take in some of the most remote parts of southern Dartmoor so are not to be undertaken lightly or without the proper clothing and equipment. Despite there being lots of features on this walk, in both good as well as in poor visibility a map and compass are essential.

Park at the western end of Venford reservoir [SX685 712]. During 2008 the Water Company undertook some significant maintenance work at the dam, building a large safety overflow to control the dam at times of high rainfall. From the car park walk uphill across the grassy slope following parallel with the road on your left to a point where the **Holne Moor Leat** ends and flows into a drain underground. Cross the road towards the open moors and follow a well-trodden path uphill with the dam lower down on your left. There are some sections deep in low lying gorse but you soon arrive at a grassy clearing and a hut circle [SX678 709] overlooking the reservoir.

From here you head westerly towards a double stone row [SX674 710] and then onto **Horn's Cross** (A) [SX669 710] with views of **Combestone Tor** down on your right by the road.

Horn's Cross

From Horn's Cross you can look west over the **O Brook valley** towards Hooten Wheals mine workings. It would be a difficult route to walk straight there so it would be sensible to consider contouring around the end of the valley to the left. Go uphill along the very clear track then branch right and contour around the end of a first gully [SX666 707] and onto the second one [SX661 706]. When you reach the second gully coming up from the river you meet a footpath also coming up from your right in the valley and crossing you to the left uphill towards Ryder's Hill.

It is at this crossroads that the 5-mile route turns left and goes uphill following the line of boundary stones all the way to **Ryder's Hill** [SX659 690] through **Wellaby Gulf** [SX659 700]. **For those on the 5-mile route, at Ryder's Hill you turn left and eastwards** following the line of boundary stones into the valley of the River Mardle and down to Hapstead Ford [SX670 692] where you meet the 10-mile route on its return journey back to Venford.

However, for those on the 10-mile route **you simply carry on at the crossroads** of the track at the top of the gullies [SX661 706] to continue contouring around to Hooten Wheals mine ruins **B** and the large demolished foundations of a rectangular building [SX655 708] and wheel pits and shafts. It might be wise not to venture into the shaft pits. They were capped by wood and corrugated iron many years ago and the wood is rotting so they might be unstable - well, *'this guide'* has never had the courage to go down into the pits and jump up and down in them! From Hooten Wheals on a clear day there are fine views over towards Exeter and east Devon.

From the mine workings head west into the gullies of Skir Gut [SX647 706] - very deep open mine gullies where you turn left and follow the mining gullies up to their head at a big pond [SX647 702] where they abruptly end.

Hapstead Ford

At the pond you can't actually see the top of Ryder's Hill to the southeast but head towards the top of the hill in the distance to the southeast. You might well see a huge granite boulder lying at the foot of the steep slopes, make your way through the tortuously long grass to this boulder and you come across quite a good path leading off to the left around the hill [SX654 696]. It's worth turning left to follow it for some respite in the long grass. This track leads you to the **crossroads junction** [SX659 697] where the 5-mile walk route comes up the hill from your left. At this point turn right and uphill along the wide path following the **Boundary Stones with 'H'** [Holne Parish] on them. This path leads you right up to the top the Ryder's Hill **C** and the Triangulation Point, another Boundary Stone as well as **Petre's Bound Stone** [SX659 690].

It is here that the 5-mile walkers branch off eastwards to Hapstead Ford but the 10-mile route heads southwest. If the weather is fine you can see the pyramid shaped spoil heap of the tip at **Red Lake** [SX464 670] in the distance. Simply head slightly to the left of this heap and drop down to the valley of the River Avon.

As you get towards the river keep a watch out for the boggy ground on your right, simply keep left and higher as you head down towards the river.

You will reach the river near the ruins of a tinner's building [SX654 669]. At the ruin turn left and follow the riverside path downstream. You soon reach a tree on the riverbank, at the base of which is the ruin of a vermin trap **D**. Continue downstream with the river on your right, and eventually you pass a fine granite clapper bridge [SX657 661] before continuing down the river to find a rather odd and out of place newly built wall with **Huntingdon Cross** [SX664 662] beside it.

Here the route goes back up to the north by following left up the **Western Wella Brook.** About 300 metres upstream on the eastern side are the remains of a small building which is known as **Keble Martin's Church** **E** [SX666 666]. The small ruins are in fact a chapel, which was built in 1909 by Keble Martin and his companions, the 6-figure grid reference being a good reason to build a church here!

From here follow the stream uphill to Huntingdon Farm ruins on your left [SX665 669]. Cross the stream and head north easterly to **Pupers Hill** [SX672 673] with its distinctive 'B' carved into the rock.

From here a short descent and up again to the north west leads you to the summit of **Snowdon** **F** [SX668 683] with views ahead and to the left of Ryder's where we were a few hours ago

Summit of Snowdon

on our walk. From Snowdon continue slightly to the right of north and down into the valley of the River Mardle to Hapstead Ford [SX670 692] where you meet the 5-mile route which has come down to join you from the valley on the left.

Hampstead Ford is very distinct with its large 'H' stone beside the track and river here. From here we head across the **Mardle** north easterly and rise the hill ahead of you. There are a number of paths going through the gorse and heather but if you head for the middle of the high ground ahead you are on the right course. This will eventually lead you to cross a good track known as the **Sandy Way** [SX679 696]. There are views ahead now that you have crested the hill, down to **Venford Reservoir** and the end of the walk.

It is easier to go to the right on the Sandy Way a short distance to a fork in the track. Fork left and this takes you downhill towards **Venford** and down to the leat which you cross. Look downhill and aim for the road to the right of the reservoir using a few of the paths and dry leats to find your way downhill to the road [SX679 696]. At the road simply turn left and walk over the dam to return to the car park and the end of the walk.

View of Pupers Hill from Huntingdon

DARTMOOR
wilderness walk 10

Dartmoor's East to West
Length: A two day walk of approximately 10 miles each day
Start: Car Park at Haytor National Park Information Centre
Grid ref: SX765 771
Difficulty: Easy to moderate on the first day due to tracks then moderate on the second day due to the remoteness.

This final walk was not included in the original articles published in the Dartmoor News because of its length and arduous nature over two days. It traverses the whole of Dartmoor from the Haytor car park Information Centre on the east side all the way across to Lydford Castle in the west. The route is split into two days with a break halfway at Bellever Car Park. The length of the walk is a total of 23 miles split into 11 miles on the first day and 12 on the second.

The halfway point at **Bellever** [SX655 771] has basic facilities, parking & a toilet, similar to the end of the second day at Lydford [SX509 847] by the Castle & Castle Inn pub. From **Haytor Car Park** [SX765 771] up and over **Haytor Quarries** [SX759 774] in a north-westerly direction to **Hound Tor**, [SX742 790] **Hameldown** [SX712 807] and **Grimspound** [SX700 808]. Then south-westerly to Bellever [SX658 773] via Challacombe [SX693 795]. On the second day the route is predominantly northwesterly all day from Bellever to Powder Mills [SX628 773] and over the open moors to cross the West Dart and on to Wilsworthy Firing Ranges and Lydford village [SX509 847].

GU...
1...
WAL...

Grid...

1. Haytor Car Park: SX765 77...
2. Hound Tor: SX742 790
3. Jay's Grave: SX732 799
4. Grimspound: SX700 808
5. Challacombe: SX693 795
6. Pizwell: SX667 784

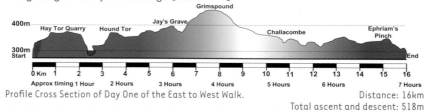

Profile Cross Section of Day One of the East to West Walk.

Distance: 16km
Total ascent and descent: 518m

War Department boundary stone

DARTMOOR
wilderness walk 10

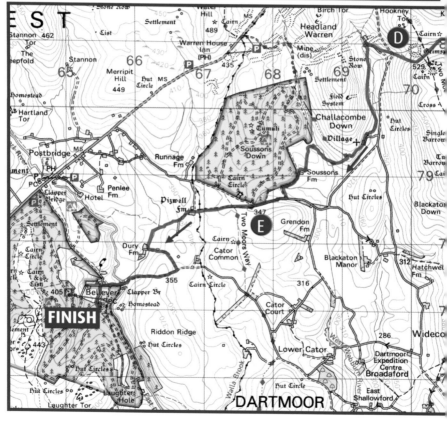

East to West walk

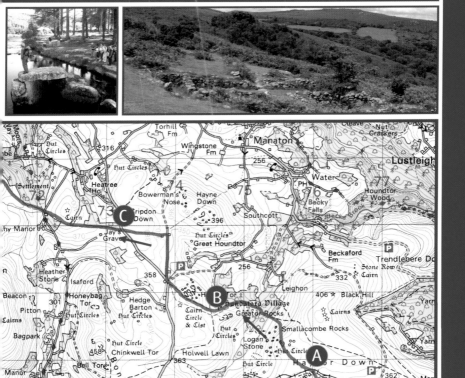

The route on the first day lies outside of the firing ranges so can be undertaken at any time. On the second day, however, the walker will pass through the Merrivale and Wilsworthy firing ranges so it is essential to check Military firing times either online at www.dartmoor-ranges.co.uk or by phone on 0800 458 4868. Firing times are also broadcast on BBC Radio Devon.

The route on the second day will cross some of the more remote areas of Dartmoor so *knowledge of using a map and compass is essential* as is also wearing suitable footwear and taking proper waterproof clothing. Crossing of a number of rivers is necessary on the second day. Some of these can rise quite quickly in wet weather so check the forecast before undertaking this section. The route also crosses quite arduous ground sometimes in quite deep grass, which can be tiring. There are also a few steep climbs so quite an ambitious day's walk.

Leave the Haytor Information Centre car park [SX765 771] and take the grassy wide path across the road to the quarries [SX759 774]. As you look uphill towards Haytor itself the path is over to the right and only goes uphill very gently. It is worth taking a detour through the gate into the quarry and through the site past the flooded areas and exit out the other side over the stile.

George Templer opened the quarries in about 1819. He was a local entrepreneur who was also responsible for the building of the **Tramway** in 1820. The quarries here lasted right up to 1858 in production but were closed due to cheaper Cornish granite. Once you exit the quarry area and climb the stile, the cutting you are in is loaded with whortleberries in the summer season. Continue out and down beside a long spoil heap leading from the quarry. If you stick to the left side going downhill and around the end of the rubble heap this will lead you to the **granite tramway A with its flanged rails.** Follow the tramway across the ancient tinners' cutting over an embankment to a junction of the route [SX757 777].

At this junction there are the remains of the granite rails and 'points' system to change the direction of the horse hauled trucks. Turn left and follow the level line of the horse drawn tramway into a shallow cutting. Once you exit from the cutting look over to the right towards a low area of rocks known as **Smallacombe Rocks** [SX754 782]. Take one of the paths to Smallacombe Rocks, passing by some well-preserved hut circles as you approach the rock piles. There are wide sweeping views away to the north and west from here, and over to **Hound Tor** [SX742 790] in the distance which is our next destination.

Continue past Smallacombe Rocks and down a steep and well-worn narrow path. This leads you down into the valley to a lovely clapper bridge [SX752 787] in the woods over the **Becca Brook,** a tributary of the River Bovey. Cross the brook and carry on up the steep path with the woods on your right. It's quite a haul to the top as you emerge out of a pedestrian gateway near to **Greator Rocks** [SX749 788]. If you walk in April then the ground over to the left is awash with bluebells making the whole hillside a glorious colour.

Carry on along the grass path towards Hound Tor [SX742 790] ahead of you. You drop down into a depression where you will locate the ruins of the famous and long abandoned **Hound Tor Mediaeval Village** **B** [SX746 787], well worth a while exploring the buildings and grain drying kilns.

Our route carries on up to the tor and through the centre of it with the high rocks either side of our path. As we crest the top of the slop our view ahead over to the northwest shows Hameldown, which is the long hill that we are going to be crossing in an hour or so.

Continue downhill towards the car park at **Swallerton Gate junction** [SX739 791] where you might be lucky to find the regular refreshment stop, open for a welcome break.

Carry on along the deceptively busy narrow lane from Swallerton Gate with its pretty cottage, formerly the **Hound Tor Inn** on your left. Don't be tempted to fork right here, but carry on the main lane in the direction of **Jay's Grave** [SX732 799] **C** only ten minutes walk away. The little grave is on your left by a gateway in the trees. There will no doubt be flowers and small gifts left on the grave of **Kitty Jay,** a local girl reputed to have been a suicide buried at the lonely spot. Go through the gate beside the grave and a footpath follows a wall on your left with the woods on your right. The views over to the left open up and down the vale into **Widecombe.** After a while you reach a point where, at the time of writing, there is located a **gigantic wooden chair sculpture** [SX723 800] - subject of much planning consent discussion, but in 2009 / 2010 it remained there, but for how long?

The footpath ends as you come to a gateway [SX720 802] at the junction of the tarmac road leading left towards Widecombe. Turn left here and then almost immediately right through a gateway signposted as a footpath and bridleway that leads up to Hameldown ridge. As you enter the gate just look along the fence to your left to a small boundary stone, dedicated to **William Pitt the Prime Minister,** one of a number of dedicated boundary stones in the area of the moor.

Our path now goes over the wall and trees on the right [SX717 803] and follows up the wide bridlepath towards the great mass of **Hameldown** - our high-point for today at about 1,500 feet above sea level. On your way to the top of the rise you can take a

Granite tramway

very short diversion to your left to view the **RAF Memorial** [SX712 807] to the crew of an aircraft, which crashed here during the last war.

Don't be tempted to turn left southwards here but continue back over to your original path, which leads you over Hameldown ridge into the dip towards **Grimspound** **D** [SX700 808] ahead of you. A visit and break here is well worth the time to explore the walls and hut circles contained within - ancient relics of inhabitants thousands of years ago. You now have a new wide view over to the west in the direction of Princetown and the high mast at **North Hessary** with the prison nestling at its base.

Our track is now downhill following the well-made granite pathway beside the little stream to the road [SX697 808] where we cross over and follow the footpath down to the right of **Headland Warren Farm** [SX693 811]. We enter the farm enclosures through a signposted gate and past the front of the farmhouse to the cattle grid exit for cars. The footpath turns right before the cattle grid and goes through a gateway and heads due south towards **Challacombe,** ancient village and settlement.

Pizwell ford

The path here follows the bottom of the valley, with evidence of tin mining gullies up to our left as well as an old field system as we enter the small settlement of Challacombe [SX693 795]. The footpath passes by the houses and through a gate across open fields and farmland towards **Soussons Farm** [SX683 790].

There is a temptation to head off right as you start to climb through the fields but the farm is clear over to your left and the path goes past the buildings and up the farm lane to the tarmac road [SX682 786].

Bellever hamlet

Turn right up the slope to the oddly-named Ephraim's Pinch **E** [SX677 785] with the trees on your right. Here the tarmac road swings sharp right but you go straight ahead down the rough trackway to the ford below **Pizwell Farm** [SX667 784]. Cross the stream up to the farm buildings and turn left along the footpath leading to Postbridge.

As you drop down into the dip by the stream, you leave the path and head downstream to the gateway of **Dury Farm** but still follow the stream all the way downhill to the road by **Bellever Bridge** [SX658 773] and the woods.

There are the ruins of the large and ancient clapper bridge here beside the new road bridge. **Simply either turn right to go to the car park in the woods via the road** or alternatively take the footpath beside the clapper bridge and go into the woods to reach today's destination at the car park [SX655 771].

Hay Tor in the distance from Bellever Tor

❙Dartmoor's East to West

Length: A two day walk of approximately 10 miles each day
Start: Car park at Haytor National Park Information Centre
Grid ref: SX765 771
Difficulty: Easy to moderate on the first day due to tracks then moderate on the second day due to the remoteness.

On the second day of the walk you start at the car park [SX655 771] where you concluded yesterday's walk.

From the car park in the woods come out into the roadway [SX655 773] and turn left in order to keep left and pass in front of the Bellever Youth Hostel on the right hand side.

Carry on up the lane to the start of the ancient and deep lane of the Lych Way ahead of you [SX653 773] - the route that corpses were taken from the east of the moorland area to Lydford Church for burial hundreds of years ago before burials were authorised at Widecombe Church.

1. Bellever Car park: SX656 77
2. Powder Mills: SX628 775
3. Broad Hole: SX591 786
4. White Barrow: SX568 793
5. River Tavy: SX540 811
6. Lydford: SX509 847

Our route for the day now follows that ancient **Lych Way;** also know as 'the way of the dead'. Ascend the deep and steep rough pathway to the gateway at the top of the lane [SX651 772]. From here on, the map shows the land as a forest but the path continues through newly-cleared ground with the stumps of trees all around. Having gone through the gate the path goes to the right uphill and around a left bend [SX650 773] as it continues uphill through the recently felled ground.

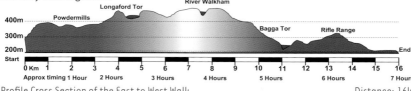

Profile Cross Section of the East to West Walk.

Distance: 16km
Total ascent and descent: 615m

Wilsworthy Ranges

DARTMOOR
wilderness walk 10

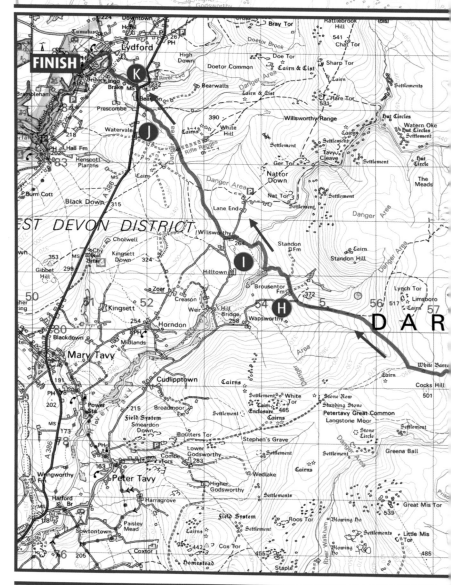

FINISH

START

G

F

We come out and across the forestry road that is used by the large Forestry Commission timber lorries and you cross the lane way [SX646 772] and over an area of open moorland. There are lovely views to the left up to **Bellever Tor** here, keep an eye out for the deer that roam the forest and moors hereabouts. Continue straight ahead as the track goes downhill with the forest on the right and then into the forest on both sides [SX643 772].

Keep a look out for a right turn, signposted by a wooden post, which is sometimes lying on the ground! Turn right here [SX639 772] for the new route of the Lych Way and to the main Postbridge Road. If you miss the right turn you simply come out on the main road but further down the hill nearer to **Cherry Brook Bridge.** The new route has been put into place to avoid the marshes near the Cherry Brook stream.

As you come out of the forest area and cross the road you go through a pedestrian gateway [SX637 776] and onto the well trod path as it goes downhill towards the marshes. Fortunately there are wooden walkway boards here to help you through the soft bits and uphill to the other side where the path bends to the left and southwesterly [SX635 778]. The route now carries on to the gateway [SX629 775] that takes you into the enclosures of **Powdermills Gunpowder** factory site **F**. The factory was built in 1844 for the production of gunpowder for the quarrying and mining industry on the moors. By 1867 and the development of dynamite the industry declined quickly. The ruins are an interesting feature well worth a deviation to explore.

The track takes you downhill to a little clapper bridge [SX628 773] over the brook and up to the solitary chimney stack where, at its rear, the path leaves the enclosure and goes out onto the open moorland again [SX626 773]. The way can be boggy here in wet weather but if you head for the high pyramid-shaped tor ahead of you the path is not too bad. The route takes you towards the tor called **Longaford** [SX615 777] and over a stile [SX618 776] in the granite wall and up to the tor.

Bellever Clapper Bridge

The views to the west and into the West Dart valley open up with **Wistman's Wood** stretching out below you in the valley.

Powdermills

We now continue down diagonally **rightwards to the river** where the Devonport Leat is taken off the main river at a purpose-built weir **G** [SX608 779]. It is possible to cross at the weir when the river is not in spate, otherwise go upstream to find suitable large boulders to cross. Once you are on the west bank the path continues uphill westerly [SX604 780] with a big depression on your right.

Avoid dropping into the lower ground on the north to the right because it is quite wet there, but instead stick to the path as it crests the ridge in front of **Lydford Tor** [SX599 780] on your right and continues westerly to a gateway [SX593 783] in the wall. The Lych Way now goes slightly upstream to **Broad Hole** [SX591 786] where there is an easy ford to get across. Carry on over the stream of the **Cowsick** and uphill on the distinct pathway [SX585 788] with the little babbling **Connies Down** water below you on your left.

Our path goes over the ridge and drops into the valley of the Walkham River and crosses near to where the **Prison Leat** is taken off the stream near a small bridge [SX574 791]. The pathway is well defined and carries on up the next hill where, at the crest, it forks right [SX565 793] and north westerly, eventually following a wall on your left which leads you all the way to **Baggator Gate** **H** and the **Army Range hut** [SX551 803]. Go through the gate and along the rough vehicle track with the small **Bagga Tor** on the right.

As you reach the end of the rough track there is a gate on your left [SX546 805] where vehicles go through onto the tarmac lane, simply carry straight on and do not go through the gateway.

Follow the wall on the left downhill and into another deep and tree lined ancient track way leading you down to the rear of **Brousentor Farm** [SX545 807] on your left. The lane carries on down a concreted track to a gate [SX544 809]. Go through the gate and bear left away from the concrete track.

Do not enter the field system on the left but carry straight on and cross over the small brook and follow it downhill into the trees where you will find it is quite a clear ancient track [SX543 811] all the way downhill around the edges of the fields and under the trees.

This track leads you to the stepping-stones ⓘ [SX540 811] over the River Tavy in **Coffin Wood.** The wood is so called because it is believed that shrouded bodies carried on packhorses were transferred to coffins here for their final journey to Lydford Church. **If you prefer there is a choice of routes here,** you could carry on over the stepping stones and up to **Higher Wilsworthy** farm but the route through the fields can be a bit confusing so it is suggested that you simply turn right and follow the Tavy upstream to the big wooden footbridge [SX539 815] and cross over there and into the main laneway which leads you, without any confusion, up to Higher Wilsworthy farm [SX535 817].

Go past the farm and out onto the tarmac road where you turn left and go downhill to a sharp right, then left hand bend with an old ruined building beside the road on the right just before you cross the small stream. Here you turn right [SX533 816] onto a footpath into the trees and go up the rough lane to the end where there is a stile; you climb over on the left without going through the gate ahead of you [SX532 818]. The path goes into the woods but soon comes out into a field, which you cross. You then go through two more fields over the stiles [SX530 822] until you come out onto the open moors [SX529 823] with a view ahead of you up to the **Wilsworthy Firing Ranges.**

There is a big wall on your right around the old fields of the ruined **Yellowmead Farm**. Ignore the farm track coming out of the gate but carry on northwards along the footpath through the heather as it takes you uphill and to a stile and bridge over the old mine le[SX526 829]. The path then carries on to the firing range building and crosses the tarmac lane used for the army lorries [SX525 832]. Cross over the laneway and start going downhill with a depression on your left, the lane leads you downhill to the wall with the trees to the gateway [SX520 839] near the new **Wilsworthy Army Camp** nestling low and out of site behind the walls ⓙ.

Go through the gate down the tarmac lane to the main **A386 Tavistock to Okehampton Road** [SX518 841]. Turn right and northwards, keeping to the grass verge on the other side of the road as you pass **Higher Beardon farm** on your left [SX518 842]. **The road is really fast here so do take care.**